Deadline–

Captain Charlie's Bataan Diary

Newspaper Reporter to Commander: Bataan, the Death March, Life in Three POW Camps—the War Story of Captain Charlie Underwood

By Charles Underwood, Jr.

Dateline—Captain Charlie's Bataan Diary
©2013 by Charles Underwood, Jr.

No part of this book may be reprinted without permission apart from review purposes. The people and characters in this book are real, and have been portrayed as accurately as possible. The author asks forgiveness for omissions, errors, or miscalculations.

Cover drawing of Captain Charlie by POW Ferdi

Published by Piscataqua Press
A project of RiverRun Bookstore
142 Fleet St
Portsmouth, NH 03801

info@riverrunbookstore.com
www.riverrunbookstore.com
www.piscataquapress.com

ISBN: 978-1-939739-02-5

Printed in the United States of America

This is dedicated to Prisoners of War, and to their families for their eternal support.

Sketch of Captain Charlie Underwood drawn in Hitachi POW Camp, North of Toyko, WWII

Timeline of Significant Events

1. May 30, 1939: Charlie hired as a reporter for Amarillo (Texas) Globe-News.

2. September 30, 1940: Charlie called up to active duty, commissioned as a Lieutenant and assigned to the Philippines on February 15, 1941.

3. December 8, 1941: Japanese bombing of Clark Air Force Base, Nichols Field, Philippines.

4. December 21, 1941: Japanese Army invades the Philippines; fighting on Luzon.

5. December 31, 1941: Pull-back into Bataan; battles fought across Bataan.

6. April 10, 1942: Bataan surrenders; start of the Death March.

7. April 15, 1942: Charlie arrives at O'Donnell POW Camp.

8. June 6, 1942: Charlie moved to Cabanatuan POW Camp.

9. March 24, 1944: Charlie embarks on the *Taikohu Maru.*

10. April 11, 1944: Charlie reaches Hitachi POW Camp, North of Tokyo.

11. August 10, 1945: Japanese Commander of POW Camp Hitachi surrenders.

12. September 6, 1945: Captain Charlie commandeers the Japanese North Train back to U.S. lines.

13. October 1945: Six Japanese guards from Hitachi Camp charged with war crimes, sent to Sugamo Prison. Tried in 1946; found guilty of "Class B and C war crimes," sentenced.

Table of Contents

Preface 1
Prologue 5
Part I 9
Chapter 1 The Early Years 11
Chapter 2 Training the Bamboo Army 29
Part II 37
Chapter 3 The Japanese Bomb Luzon 39
Chapter 4 MacArthur's Plans, and Initial Probe Landings by the Japanese ... 47
Chapter 5 The Invasion of Luzon 55
Chapter 6 War Plan Orange—Being Pushed from All Sides 65
Chapter 7 The Siege of Bataan 71
Chapter 8 The Japanese Breakthrough and the Fall of Bataan 89
Part III 95
Chapter 9 The Death March 97
Chapter 10 In Captivity: Prison Camps on Luzon, Philippines 107
Part IV 123
Chapter 11 The Voyage on the *Taikoku Maru* 125
Chapter 12 Prison Camp Hitachi 129
Chapter 13 Charlie as Camp Mess Officer 163
Chapter 14 Christmas Season 1944 and Red Cross Packages 173
Chapter 15 Spring 1945 Contact from the U.S. Air Corps 177
Chapter 16 The Surrender of the Japanese at #8 Camp Hitachi 181
Chapter 17 Commandeering the Train 189
Chapter 18 The War Crime Charges 201
Chapter 19 The Transition 207
Chapter 20 Interviews 213
Bibliography 223
Appendix I: Sample War Crimes Charges 227
Appendix II: Captain Underwood's report on nutrition in the Camp ... 239
Appendix III: Japanese Surrender Documents 255
Acknowledgments 259
About the Author 261

List of Maps, Photographs and Artifacts

1.	Map of the Philippines Islands and Japan	2
2.	The Reporter	15
3.	Charlie's old car	16
4.	News report of Charlie's car	17
5.	Enjoying the Philippines	28
6.	Charlie's Car after gunfire	53
7.	Map of Japanese invasion on Luzon Island, Philippines	58
8.	Map of Bataan positions	73
9.	Quinaun Point	81
10.	Telegram of capture	98
11.	Camp O'Donnell	118
11B.	Newspaper headline of capture	119
12.	POW postcards	120
12B.	Japanese and Filipino money	121
13.	The POWs of Camp Hitachi	129
14.	POW I.D. photos of American officers of Camp Hitachi	138
15.	Hitachi Camp diagram	139
16.	Sketch of Captain Underwood by fellow POW	154
17.	Photo of sick bay in Camp Hitachi	161
18.	Burial services for POWs	174
19.	Food drop news article	185
20.	Photograph of Colonel Charlie and Mrs. Underwood	211
21.	Medals	220
22.	Funeral	221

Preface

There are thousands of U.S. soldiers who never have been properly recognized for their contributions in defending the Philippines during the outbreak of World War II. This is a story of one of them. Charlie Underwood was a newspaper reporter when he was called up as a young infantry officer to active duty and sent to the Philippines. This is his story—in one year he went from reporter to infantry commander.

At the beginning of World War II, on December 7, 1941, the Philippines was bombed by the Japanese just hours after Pearl Harbor, and days later, invaded by the Japanese Army. Captain Charlie fought in the Luzon and Bataan campaigns until the fateful U.S. capitulation with the Japanese 14th Imperial Army in April of 1942. He survived the infamous Death March, and spent three and a half years as a prisoner of war; the last POW camp was north of Tokyo.

The Philippines consist of hundreds of islands which form a natural barrier between Japan and the rich resources of Southeast Asia. Most Filipinos live on Luzon, the largest island. Its capital, Manila, is located on the waterfront of a deep harbor.

Preface

In 1941, the Philippines formed the westernmost United States military outpost, five thousand miles from Pearl Harbor, and over seven thousand miles from San Francisco. (See Figure 1) By contrast, Manila is only seventeen hundred miles from Japan. The Philippines campaign was America's first involvement in the Pacific War against the vast military forces of the Japanese Empire. The Japanese had already conquered Manchuria, Korea, Burma, and parts of China and Thailand. Even after the attack on Pearl Harbor, President Franklin D. Roosevelt saw the war in Europe, and stopping Hitler, as the more immediate threat and committed his war effort there. American soldiers stationed in the Pacific paid dearly for that decision.

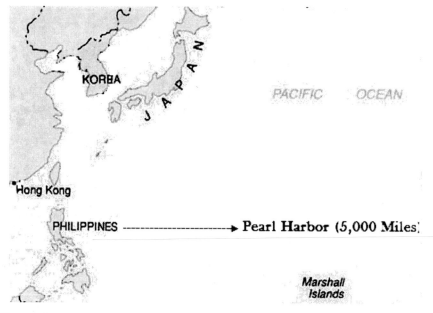

Figure 1

This account describes the fighting on Luzon, Bataan, and the subsequent Death march. It also illustrates the ordeals of daily life as a captive in three prison camps, with special attention to life at the Hitachi Camp in Japan. It is one of the few accounts written about Americans in a Japanese POW camp.

The sources for this work are truly unique. Chief among them is Charlie's 75-page monograph, *The Defense of Luzon and Bataan & December 1941 – April 1942,* written in 1947. It details the battles on Luzon, the ninety-nine day siege and fall of Bataan. It is based on his own firsthand account as a commander, plus interviews with other leaders who fought there. Charlie fought alongside key officers, such as Captain Tom Dooley, aide to General Wainwright (later overall commander); Major Joe Chabot, G-2 to Wainwright; and Captain Art Christensen, G-2 South Force G-2, under General Parker and A.M. Jones. In addition, company commanders Captain John Pray and Lieutenant Gene Conrad of the 31st Infantry, who fought in the critical battles at Layac Junction; First Lieutenant with the enemy in the south; and Lieutenant R.D. "Tex" Evans, who came from Fort McKinley with the Philippine Scouts. Charlie also drew on material from the original war reports of the operations of North, (Corp I), and South Force (Corp II). A second source were interviews with Japanese officers while he was held in captivity.

Preface

Another major source of material for this work came from his affidavits filed with the War Crime Commission attesting to atrocities committed by Japanese prison guards. Charlie was determined to see a measure of justice meted against his brutal Japanese camp guards for committing atrocities against American and Allied POWs.

In this book, people, events and locations are identified as fully as possible, but there are instances where only a first name or nickname could be confirmed, or only an approximate location identified.

Prologue
Fort Sam Houston, Texas, National Cemetery

On the morning of November 23, 2006, the sun felt warm over the manicured lawn at Fort Sam Houston National Cemetery in San Antonio, Texas. A slight breeze fluttered which was welcomed by the mourners attending a military funeral.

In the first row, the elderly widow sat weeping. She was here to bury her Charlie, her husband of over fifty years. The other mourners had come to pay their last respects to a friend and relative. He was a patriot, a survivor of Bataan and the Death March and had spent three and half years as a prisoner of war. He was a soldier who above all demanded and got a measure of justice for war atrocities.

Most mourners were seated in folding chairs. The rows of chairs extended twenty rows back. In the back was the overflow, mostly men, late arrivals, or those who preferred to stand to absorb the somber mood of this mid-November day.

Prologue

One of those standing was the old Colonel Johnny Olson, dressed in a tattered World War II uniform, here to mourn his lost friend. On one sleeve of his uniform was the Philippine Campaign insignia. On his collar was the rank of colonel. He had known the widow for over fifty years, his buddy Charlie even longer. He could not hold back the tears. They had fought on Bataan and were later POWs together. The colonel's name tag was faded but it still spelled out "Olson." Now he was the last survivor of their group from 1941, and he felt very lonely.

Behind the grave site was a thin blacktop road. A car pulled into view as a belated mourner arrived. Another veteran opened the door and got out. He wore a dark-tweed topcoat rather than a uniform.

He had flown overnight to make the service. As it was a pleasant day, he took off his coat. He nodded to Olson and walked right up and stood before the seated widow. He spoke low with a strong Dutch-English accent. Trying to catch his breath, he bent over to console her. As he leaned forward, his neck revealed a pattern of ugly scars, a row of round, whitish blotches, caused by repeated torture many years past. He knew Charlie had endured his share, perhaps even more.

"Missus,"—his eyes began tearing—"in September of '45, a month after the Japanese surrender when the war was supposedly over, we were still POWs north of Tokyo, and Captain Charlie commandeered a train through Japan. He rescued me and my entire unit. We are alive today because of him. May he now rest in peace, one truly deserved."

His lips quivered. He wanted to say more but could not find words. The widow held her hand out in thanks. He nodded and moved aside, finding an empty chair nearby.

There was stillness for a moment until the rhythmic sound of horse hooves was heard in the distance, coming closer on the blacktop road. An honor guard of military men and horses slowly pulled a caisson with a flagdraped casket on the wagon.

All watched in silence as the military funeral detail slowly marched by. The men in their formal dress-blue uniforms, were impeccable in their dress and manner. A single horse was trailing the rear of the wagon, a pair of boots reversed in its stirrups—a custom reserved for the honored personnel. At an appointed time the young officer stopped. Solemnly he called his burial detail to attention. The burial team lifted the coffin and gently placed it on the pallet near the gravesite.

Around the casket, soldiers lined up and with precision, aimed seven rifles skyward. The gunfire ripped the stillness of the morning—three times for a total of twenty one shots. It was a

Prologue

longheld military tradition dating back to the Civil War era, when three volleys signified a ceasefire to both sides in order to clear the dead. On this sunny November morning, it was the last time the sound of rifle fire would be heard near Charlie Underwood. That, in itself, was strange because years before it had been so much of his daily routine for one hundred days in combat on Luzon and in Bataan in 1941 and 1942.

A lone bugler sounded Taps, signifying a final restful sleep for the warrior. Then the funeral officer presented the United States flag to the widow. A final salute ended the tribute. The funeral detail was called to attention. There was a moment of silence, and, then they slowly marched off to the right, as the clanging of horse hoofs faded into the distance.

Part I

The Early Years and Events Leading Up to the War

Chapter 1 | The Early Years

Charlie Underwood was raised on a farm near Atchison, Kansas. The farm produced wheat, barley and dairy products. Both he and his older brother Ernie were faced with plenty of chores to do before school and worked in the fields after school. This was expected from farm kids in the late 1920s and '30s. Charlie attended school at a two-room schoolhouse and, like most in rural areas, rode his own pony there and back. At the start of sixth grade, he fell off his horse and broke his collar bone. He could not attend school. Emma, his mother, who had graduated from the Lawrence Finishing School home-schooled him until his injury healed. She taught him grammar, writing and spelling. When he returned the next fall in seventh grade, he won the district's spelling bee.

Several years later, his father, Ernest, was elected State Representative for rural Kansas. The family moved to Topeka, the nearby state capital, when his father was appointed to the highway commission the next year. Topeka was a small town.

The Early Years

Charlie excelled in both academics and sports. In high school, he kept up his grades, was a member of the debate club, and lettered in basketball and track. Ernie, eight years his senior, had just started a construction company. He hired Charlie, first as a part-time water boy who brought refreshments to the workers, and then as a helper to load and off-load supplies from the work truck. Soon this tall and lanky boy could outwork most of the men. His mother kept him focused on his books and kept tight rein on his academic work.

After high school, Charlie was accepted into the University of Missouri's School of Journalism. In the summers, he worked as a student-reporter for the *Amarillo Globe-News* newspaper in Texas. In those days in the late 1930's, before television, city newspapers were the chief source for daily news. Gene Howe, editor and one of the paper's founders, was a legend in Texas journalism. Gene took Charlie under his wing. He had a talent for mentoring reporters. His motto was, "be accurate, fast and brief." He was tough in his demands. Stories he didn't like ended up in the redo box. One exercise that Gene employed to help novices hone their skills was the five minute drill. "Write a news story in five minutes! Yes, with a typewriter." This was some achievement for any reporter, thought Charlie. Charlie had to learn speed typing. Using only his index fingers he practiced typing each day by pecking out letters on the typewriter. By the end of summer, he had mastered the skill. He was quite pleased when Gene said on his final day, "Well,

I expect you to perfect it when you come back next summer." He left the *Globe* that day beaming with delight! Charlie corresponded with Gene for many years until his death in the mid 1950's.

In college, his older brother Ernie suggested he enroll in Reserve Officer Training. Ernie was a naval reservist as a Seabee. Charlie wore glasses and had to settle for the Army.

After graduation, Charlie's first job was back at the *Amarillo Globe-News* as a reporter, writing ads, which taught him the value of great one-liners. Customers paid for each word and Charlie made it brief. After the second day, his partner called in sick, Charlie stayed and worked both shifts. He wanted to prove his worth. He covered double shift for the department for over a week, producing twice the volume of anyone else. Charlie was good at his craft. With ads came money and he soon received recognition for his work and eager attitude.

Two significant events occurred that year in Amarillo. His first was when he covered the stabbing in downtown Amarillo. Late one Friday evening, he was writing ads, when the police radio sounded reports of a downtown brawl resulting in a stabbing.

He had been on the job only a month, but was very interested in covering this story as a first big break. The night editor strutted in with a very serious look on his face, and said, "Charlie, you're the

The Early Years

only reporter here. I'm gonna send you downtown, but just get the facts and stay out of the way. And, for God's sake, don't you get stabbed."

He rushed out with the photographer to the bar district. He interviewed the police and a witness and "got the facts" right off the street. He wrote the story and turned it in to the editor right away. To Charlie's amazement, it was "good for print," and made the next edition's front page of the *Amarillo Globe-News*. From that day on, the regular reporters considered him "one of the gang."

Charlie would keep these friends, during the early war years and throughout most of his military career. In stories about the Philippines preparing for war, they gave him top billing. Sometimes they would take a few editorial liberties with letters he sent to friends in Amarillo, and his personal information would end up in the newspaper. Such was the case with his old car. Charlie wrote to a buddy about finding a sub-section in army regulations that permitted him to ship his personal car to the Phillipines—a 1939 Ford, worth a sum of $400, still carrying Texas state plates. To an Amarillo reporter, that was a big deal. Soon that story was seen in print in both *The Amarillo Globe-News* and in the *Topeka Daily Capital* back in his hometown.

Figure 2: The young reporter for the *Amarillo Globe-News 1939*

Figure 3: Captain Charlie's '39 Ford, his pride and joy

DAILY CAPITAL

Takes His Car With Him To the Philippine Islands

Charles Underwood, son of Ernest Underwood, an official in the State Highway Department, claims to be the only American Army officer in the Philippines with a car with a Texas license.

Young Underwood, who left Topeka to attend the University of Missouri's school of journalism and then assume a position with the Amarillo (Texas) Globe - News, wrote last week from Manila that his car arrived in the Islands after a two-and-one-half-months journey from San Francisco.

Underwood says that work in the Philippines is very interesting because of the defense drive there. He reports that Army officers are working twice as hard as they did in peace time.

The young reserve officer was in a party recently which escorted Mr. and Mrs. Henry Luce about the Island. Mr. Luce is the editor of Life and Time magazines, and Mrs. Luce is the well-known woman playwright who publishes under her maiden name, Clare Booth.

UNDERWOOD AND HIS CAR

Respect No Standings Records

From purely circumstantial evidence, it looks as though Uncle Sam is trying to transport his Texas Panhandle boys as far from their native Plains as possible. But they are still breaking records wherever they go.

Perhaps the most unusual out of this week's crop of mail belongs to Charlie Underwood, a former member of the Globe-News family (advertising department) who is now with the U. S. armed forces in Manila, Philippine Islands.

"Submitted is my claim, with photo for proof, of taking an Amarillo car and Potter County license farther than any other of our local citizens," he writes. "My car came this past week-end, more than two and a half months after I left it in San Francisco.

"Of course, we have to get Manila plates and such, so I wanted to get this picture while some of the Texas atmosphere remained.

"I'm liking it over here a lot. Although we are working about three times as hard as has been the custom in the Philippines, the work is interesting and for the most part pleasant. And I had a swell trip over here.

"That, and the fact there's many side trips as well as exploring Manila itself is making this stay mighty nice. No one here seems to know how long we'll be here—if it will be more than two years or not. This depends a lot on the international conditions, I think.

"We are still in the midst of a rainy season here, which would turn the Panhandle into a small sea. It is the only time of constant moisture and lasts from middle of June into October. Then it is dry again until this time next year they tell me.

CHARLIE UNDERWOOD

"Except the small European-American colony, Manila is almost sans white women. All the army and navy wives and families have been sent back, or are in the process of being sent back, to the States. But as they say about the little 'brown sisters'—'These girls sure have a healthy tan, don't they?'

"To capitalize on the practice blackout which was staged here last week, the local press put on some advertising specials. Most outstanding was a double truck of about 2 by 6 ads with every other one a reverse.

"Engraving costs are very cheap and many of the ads make use of all the modern practices known. So you can see the fourth estate is pretty much on its toes. I've picked up a couple of good ideas already. In my work I come in contact with many of the local press.

"Also one night I was in an Army-Navy party to escort Claire Booth Luce (Mrs. Life-Time, as well as being pretty well known, of course, in her own right) and a young fellow White, who had been called back to the States by Time to handle their Far Eastern desk. These two joined Mr. Luce and they took the clipper back. But we fairly showed them the town 'as an average soldier or sailor sees it.'

"I often wonder how the war scares, conscription, etc., are affecting business and in turn advertising back in the States, particularly Amarillo."

A former Kansan, Underwood worked in the editorial department four summers while attending the University of Missouri School of Journalism. He came here immediately after graduation. He was called into service due to his reserve officer status.

Figure 4: Charlie's car makes the news

The Early Years

The *Amarillo Globe-News* treated him as though he were merely on a leave of absence. Part of one interesting newspaper column was taken from a letter he wrote about meeting the famous *Life* and *Time* magazine editor Clare Boothe Luce.

Later, when war in the Pacific was imminent, all letters were subject to military censorship. If Charlie wrote about the Philippines in his personal letters, he would find out weeks later that it had been printed in the newspaper back in Amarillo. The threat of hostilities with Japan was a tinderbox that got front page headlines. He was careful what he wrote.

In Amarillo, the second significant occurrence happened in 1939 when he met Geneva Sullivan, who went by the nickname "Jimmie"—the woman he would marry after the war and would remain with for the rest of his life. He met her through a friend. She was on a blind date with Charlie's older brother, who was visiting. Jimmie and Charlie were closer in age and hit it off.

She was gorgeous, and they clicked together immediately. Jimmie loved to dance and was a regular at the Friday night "dance hops". But Charlie was sports-minded. Sometimes he cut the dancing short to make the last few innings of the Amarillo Triple-A baseball game.

*   *   *

Charlie had been a reporter for over a year when, in February of 1940, an official Army letter directed him to active duty as a lieutenant. He was stationed first at Fort Sam Houston, Texas, assigned to the 2nd Infantry Division. He was told to prepare for a trip to the Philippines, and his assignment to the 31st Infantry. His regiment would bolster up the defenses for that island nation, to counter the warlike threat of the Japanese Empire. The unit proceeded to San Francisco by train.

When he arrived at the docks in San Francisco, his transport ship was still loading supplies. The men had a two day pass. Charlie and his fellow officers stayed together in small groups. The first night, they made sure the troops were settled in, and then they played cards, their favorite pastime. Usually, the game was bridge. They refrained from poker or any form of betting.

Charlie befriended Lieutenant Earl Short, who had been an enlisted clerk for General MacArthur. He cut a spotless appearance, and was a very efficient officer, knowledgable of Army regulations. Like Charlie, he was originally from a farm in Kansas, so they had a lot to talk about.

Another friend was Lieutenant Gene Conrad, who had been a fullback on the South Carolina college football team. Like Charlie, Gene had gone through Reserve Officers' Training Corps (ROTC). Although his size was intimidating, he was always a gentleman,

The Early Years

and a team player. Gene had a reputation as the "go-to guy" in a clutch situation since his college days.

Another Lieutenant, Matt Dobrinic, was more serious. He was an ardent student of guerrilla war tactics and a resourceful bridge player. Lieutenant John Pray was a personable, eager type, used to succeeding in every task. Like Charlie, both were tall and slim. John and Charlie ran track in college. Soft-spoken John was a "miler." In that era, the major running event was the mile. Runners in every country were close to breaking the four-minute mile. Track stars were a news item and followed by thousands of fans.

As for 2nd Lieutenant Tex Evans, he was the kid of the group, new graduate of Officer Candidate School (OCS), which was a ninety-day training program to produce junior officers. Tex, age 19, was about a year and a half younger than the rest. He had not been a college athlete either. Instead he had worked on a cattle ranch in his home state of Texas. Since Texas was Charlie's new home, they had that in common. He looked up to Charlie as an older brother. The other officers saw Charlie as a very determined man. Charlie stood six feet tall, was in very good "runner" shape, and had a commanding voice. They also appreciated his ability to retain facts. When one first met Charlie, foremost was his unnerving stare. When his eyes fell upon you, they stared through you. As a group, all these men would become solid military leaders.

After their first evening of leave in San Francisco, Charlie's group organized a tour of San Francisco's highlights. The city of San Francisco welcomed the soldiers. Local citizens rewarded the patriotism of a man in uniform with half-price drinks, meals and taxi rides. Some bars provided beer on the house.

Charlie loved the Fisherman's Wharf. He found the tourist shops and restaurants very friendly, and it was festive to be right on the water. Sightseeing was fun. People asked to take photos standing next to a serviceman, and the soldiers were happy to oblige.

Charlie and his colleagues set sail by Navy transport a day later. San Francisco faded like a setting sun, and they arrived in Manila in April 1941. Charlie was processed into the 31st Infantry, and was given his assignment to command an armored tank company. The tanks had been delayed by the shortage of transport ships. Explaining the situation was Captain Art Christensen. Christensen, a few years older, was a skillful leader and a fair officer. He assisted Charlie in finding a nice apartment and another temporary assignment while he waited. They would be dear friends for the rest of their lives.

* * *

The Early Years

Charlie Joins the Military Police, Post of Manila, Philippine Department

"The 808th was probably the first Military Police Company to come into physical contact with the enemy in WWII." *Manila MPs—the 808th, 1941"* written by LTC Charlie C. Underwood, published in *Army Magazine,* 1953.

In late 1941, Captain W.E.W. Farrell, of the 808th Military Police Battalion, was expanding his unit in preparation for hostilities. New duties required that MPs undergo additional training in counterinsurgency, as well as other MP functions. Farrell had been given a free hand to select three or four new officers and was tasked to raise his unit's strength from 65 to 180 men. The first officer he selected was Charlie.

Captain Farrell, a West Point graduate, was a man of keen intellect. He came from a military family; his dad and younger brother were also in the Army. Captain Farrell's position also made him the provost marshal (PM) of Manila, the head guy for law enforcement. Charlie was his first platoon leader. The two hit it off well. Charlie was more outgoing; Farrell, who was older than Charlie, was more reflective. Farrell saw Charlie as a natural leader and later wanted him to transfer permanently into the MPs. They were both of the same faith and, as war loomed, attended the same church. They played bridge together, with Captain Art Christensen. Christensen had a military intelligence background, a similar mindset, and fit in easily. Charlie seemed to know everybody and had a relaxed relationship with his friends of the press. On the streets of Manila, conscious of the possibility that he might resume a journalism career after the war, Charlie would wave hello to an occasional reporter, while many officers opposed them altogether and walked the other way to avoid them.

Charlie's first task was to recruit 100 men. He accepted the recruits on a trial basis. The training was tough and he chose only the best. As a result, they ended up with a cracker-jack unit. Retired Philippine Scout Non-Commissioned Officers (NCOs) were also recalled from retirement.

The old NCOs, most with over twenty years of service, were proud to be recalled but not thrilled to hear about the duties such as walking a beat or traffic management. The old boys wanted to "go fight Japs," Charlie recalled later. When "other duties" besides policing were explained, such as hunting out saboteurs, most stuck with it and went through the training. Soon, they were given their first mission. Charlie was ordered to investigate whether Japanese sympathizers were shining signal lights at night from a hill outside Manila to an unknown boat. Charlie collected a dozen men into two vehicles on a dark night; when they got there, shots were exchanged. That was all that was needed. Having received a

The Early Years

baptism by fire, the retired Filipino scouts were now honored to be selected to serve.

Charlie got along well with them and had the same perspective since he was trained as an infantry line officer, not a military policeman. He decided to make the best of the situation and prove his usefulness. First, he handled all the court-martials with ease due to his writing skills, then all the company admin. Captain Farrell praised his work, relishing the day he could rejoin the 31st Infantry. Unbeknownst to Charlie, Farrell also sent favorable reports to his seniors about Charlie's capabilities as his interim replacement. Quickly, Charlie became the executive officer (XO) and assistant provost marshal of Manila. He was made acting commander after Farrell transferred. Captain Farrell then became S-2 (Intelligence Operation Officer) of the 31st Infantry and fought on Bataan. Sadly, he later died from suffocation in a non-ventilated hold of a cargo freighter while being transferred to Japan as a POW.

In 1940-41, the 808th Military Police shared the other end of their building with the 31st Infantry; at times the units trained together as well as kept abreast of their respective training activities. Charlie did so to stay abreast of infantry tactics.

One of his first duties as an MP was escorting drunken soldiers off the streets of Manila and back to their respective units. Most of these soldiers were well-behaved and just wanted to let off some steam. On weekends, his unit's mission had him walking the red-light district. Of course, there were a few brawls, and the MPs transported their fair share to nearby Sternberg Army Hospital for the treatment of cuts and bruises and other medical aid.

On his rounds Charlie was accompanied by a twenty-five-year veteran MP sergeant. This crusty character, and teller of many tales, taught him everything. There was never a dull night. One evening the sergeant and Charlie went down to a notorious red-light hangout to investigate an earlier incident. When they arrived the club was quiet; too quiet.

They were about to sit at a table, when the sergeant took out his nightstick and threw it across the room toward a customer sitting at the bar. Hit him right on the head! Charlie thought the old sergeant had finally snapped. The customer lurched over, stunned. Then, *crash*—down dropped the beer bottle he was preparing to throw with his hidden left hand. The sergeant had uncanny instincts, learned through years of experience. Restoring peace and rounding up drunken GIs became quite an education for Charlie from Kansas.

Charlie realized how lucky he was to be assigned to the Military Police Unit. He patrolled the whole island, pretty much as he saw fit. He commanded a reliable, handpicked unit eager for duties. By the time war broke out, his MPs formed a solid team, able to

The Early Years

perform round-the-clock mobile reconnaissance throughout the island. As a special unit, he later attended senior-level tactical and staff meetings, where about pending war plans were discussed.

Charlie's new life in the Philippines was quite a change from stateside. The Philippines had plush blue skies, an aquamarine ocean and sandy beaches. He had his car and a small apartment at the Army-Navy Club on Manila Bay. The Army-Navy Club had a restaurant, a game room, several bars, a bowling alley and a swimming pool. The rooms were furnished and with them came a houseboy, named Juan. Juan, age eighteen, stood barely five-foot-four, and was a very hard worker and room service was free, but Charlie always tipped Juan the equivalent of a dollar or two each month. Juan was so proud to be working for U.S. officers! When Charlie's duties extended late into the night, Juan would have hot coffee or soup ready when he returned. He was like a little spark plug. He wanted badly to be in the Philippine Army and begged Charlie to help him enlist. One night Charlie used him as a driver while making security rounds in his own auto. They drove around the Army bases of Luzon checking the billets and areas for saboteurs. Nothing much happened that night, but it gave Juan great pride and a sense of purpose. As they went through small villages, Juan introduced Charlie to each mayor—key contacts which would prove useful in the coming weeks. Charlie later found Juan an assignment in the training of the national forces.

Within the regiment, Lieutenant Charlie Underwood found himself in charge of many tasks. He was especially adept at the technical writing of legal affidavits for court-martials. This was good practice for the war crimes reports to come later, as well as learning more about military law. Charlie found writing military reports similar to writing newspaper articles in that one focused just on the facts.

One sunny Saturday morning, the regimental colonel summoned him into his office. He had read a small article about a Luau that Charlie had written. "I'm in trouble," Charlie thought, "here comes a dressing-down." The colonel said, "Charlie, many of my basic line officers can't even write a damn paragraph; we're putting you on the training schedule to teach a writing class." Charlie spent the next few Saturday mornings teaching Composition 101. Students were fellow officers and senior NCOs. It was probably good for his career, too. He made captain at the end of the year.

Figure 5: Enjoying the Philippines

Chapter 2 | Training the Bamboo Army

"It takes about a year to fully train a soldier for combat with qualified instructors. We had about ninety days, and our instructors came out of our hide." —Charlie Underwood

On July 26, 1941, a new command in the Philippines was created, the United States Armed Forces Far East (USAFFE), under retired General Douglas MacArthur. He was then Major General, but was recalled to duty with the rank of Lieutenant General. MacArthur had long served in the Philippines as a U.S. general and was highly respected there. He had been modernizing the Filipino Army. MacArthur addressed the American soldiers and revealed his plan for creating a new American–Filipino Command. The General spoke with the command presence of Caesar, recalled Charlie in his notes.

The Army Organizational command scheme in December 1940 had at the top level USAFFE Command Headquarters, commanded by General MacArthur. Under him, two commanders of two-star rank led Corps I and Corps II. Within each corps were two or three divisions led by commanders of one-star rank. Next were the division's three regiments commanded by colonels. Within a regiment, there were usually three battalions led by lieutenant colonels, each having at least four companies with commanders with the rank of captain, which contained four platoons, each led by an officer with the rank of lieutenant.

Mobilization of the ten Filipino divisions began. All active military forces of the Philippine Commonwealth were to be inducted into the Army of the United States to create a joint American-Filipino Army. American officers and noncommissioned officers were sent or, in Charlie's case, detailed for short periods to the Philippine Army units, to teach combat tactics.

Overnight, the U.S. cadre began running a basic training course using only the resources, officers, and NCOs they had available. It was through this effort that the Philippine Army received any training. So they were, at least, partially prepared for the rigors of war.

Captain Christensen was in charge of one part of their training. He knocked on Charlie's door late one Friday and asked him to take a look at his obstacle course. Charlie took his houseboy, Juan, out to try the course that very evening. He found, to his dismay, that the obstacles had not taken into account the average size of the smaller Filipino trooper. At one station where men were supposed to swing over an object, Juan could not even reach the bar. He was too short, and necessary modifications had to be made. Barriers were lowered just in the nick of time to create a manageable versus an impossible challenge on the obstacle course.

Other problems could not be resolved so easily. Most equipment was outdated; the Enfield rifle was old, had structural issues, and required modification because it jammed. One unit commander flatly refused to use the rifle on the front lines. Others found that a simple thing like a bamboo rod cleared the shell from the casing, and put the rifle to fair use, at least, for a while.

The biggest problem was the language barrier. There were dozens of dialects in this country, and U.S. instructors had to exercise endless patience to make themselves understood. This was often more important than teaching tactics. Many Filipino soldiers did not understand simple phrases such as "dig a foxhole" or "fire and movement," much less "covering fire" and other common military terms. When instructors used these terms, they were met with blank Filipino stares. Each term or concept had to be demonstrated and reviewed often.

Other times their training had a high risk factor. One of the duties Charlie dreaded most was the training on the mortars. These muzzle–loaded cannons have a toploaded tube in which a round slides down until detonated. In the event of a misfire, it was the officer's responsibility to ensure the removal of the "dud" round that had failed to fire—something that happened to Charlie his first time on the range. The problem with a dud was that it could "cook off" and detonate at any second while the round was still chambered. Sometimes a mortar round ignited just as the mortar tube was being lowered to extract it; one could only hope a soldier's face was not in the way as the round blasted off downrange.

Misfires were frequent because of expired ammunition from World War I, which were the only munitions available. There was also a lack of spare parts for the machine guns, which caused them to jam within minutes. Unit commanders were therefore disinclined to use them.

The only communication equipment were portable radios at a regimental level. This left our commanders on the front lines without immediate communication. "We had to make use of runners to carry tactical messages," recalled Charlie. This created delays and interfered with fluidity of movement—a key tactical principle of war. From firsthand experiences, it was known that during some battles, regiments and battalions could not be communicated with, and were kept in the dark as to the plans and movement of adjacent units.

Transportation was limited for the movement of equipment or troops. They used horses, trucks and commercial buses. Overall, the dearth of munitions and equipment was startling. Except for an ordnance depot at Little Baguio in Bataan, there were no large munitions caches in Bataan when the war broke out. Individual field equipment was lacking in many essential areas. The Army tropical helmet, made from a hard paper paste, offered little head protection and reflected the sun. Supplies of blankets, shelter half-tents, and boots were woefully short, and many Filipino soldiers went barefoot.

Philippine Army soldiers often carried all their possessions on bamboo poles, slept on bamboo mats, and had to use short bamboo rods to clear their Enfield rifles. That was the reason people used the mocking name "Bamboo Army." Few Filipino companies participated in live-fire training exercises. Those that did were found to be very jittery and trigger-happy. When the soldiers heard a noise, they would shoot their rifles without confirmation of a target. They acted like a rag-tag, undisciplined army. U.S. instructors had all they could do to manage the concept of coordinated firepower. On a beach exercise instructors evacuated local civilians to avoid an errant round exploding near a passerby.

Filipino recruits, proud to defend their country, were eager to learn and become skilled soldiers; however there was not enough time. The Philippine Department, with its Division of the 26th Regiment, Philippine Scout (PS) units was the only unit capable of combat on Luzon (besides the 31st American Infantry) when the war broke out. The 26th engaged the brunt of the Japanese

Northern attack and thus freed up other units to pull back and mount a defense.

In the northern campaign, Filipinos volunteered to drive openair buses to help reposition U.S. and Filipino troops. The problem was that under any hostile fire, the drivers ran away. Charlie tried to constrain their impulses to flee by sending out armed MP escort vehicles for protection.

For Charlie, the precursor to war came the third week in November, 1941. That week the main roads were jammed with cars and buses carrying Japanese citizens to ships returning to Tokyo. Orders had been given from Tokyo to evacuate Japanese citizens living in the Philippine; war was imminent.

The hostilities, however, had their roots in events that had occurred many years earlier. The Japanese failed to ratify the Treatment of Prisoners of War Act at the 1929 Geneva War Convention. Instead, Imperial Japan pledged adherence only to the ruthless and outdated Samurai Bushido Code; surrender was considered a disgrace and prisoners were treated cruelly. Such belief was put into practice when they invaded Burma and eastern China in the 1930s and slaughtered helpless Burmese and Chinese, leading to what history calls the Rape of Nanking in 1937.

President Roosevelt froze Japanese bank assets in the U.S. On November 26, 1941, all U.S. military leaves were canceled in the Philippines. At the request of the Japanese consulate, two Japanese passenger ships in Manila Harbor began loading more than two thousand Japanese citizens working in Manila for return to Japan. Army Chief-of-Staff George C. Marshall cabled General MacArthur that war was probably imminent.

Civilians Prepare for Defense

With Charlie's headquarters located on Dewey Boulevard, he had a ringside seat to the defense preparations in Manila. A civilian defense organization had been established by the mayor. Air raid warning systems was installed in Manila and other larger cities; Charlie remembered the air raid drills occurring at inconvenient times. One day, an air raid drill occurred at siesta time during the Filipinos' traditional midday sleep, a habit they had adopted from the Spaniards who had colonized them centuries earlier. Sleepy Philippine citizens spilled into the streets when they heard the warning siren, staggering around in confusion. When they realized it was merely a drill, they briefly got a little indignant; but they were quick to realize it was for their own safety.

A food ration plan for the entire Commonwealth was being planned by the Philippine government. Practice blackouts were held in Manila in late November. Food supplies were being accumulated and hidden as temporary measures. All such activities were coordinated to give the assurance of a sound national defense plan. As allies of America, Filipinos believed that the United States would not let their country fall into Japanese hands.

Forces on Corregidor, the island protecting Manila Harbor, and North and South Luzon forces were placed on alert for surprise Japanese attacks.

Part II

The War

Chapter 3 | The Japanese Bomb Luzon

The morning of December 8, 1941, Charlie heard in disbelief the news that the Japanese air force had bombed Pearl Harbor, Hawaii. That set the island on alert. He kept close by both phone and radio for more news or further instructions from higher command. At lunch time he drove onto Dewey Boulevard and saw overhead in the distance a formation of planes; shortly after, he heard the low rumble of bombing. Black smoke drifted from the direction of Clark Field. Charlie immediately returned to the Dewey Station and ordered his men to standby.

Despite the warning represented by the attack at Pearl Harbor, nine hours later the Japanese pilots of the 11th Air Fleet bombed the Philippines and caught Clark Airfield off guard. Two squadrons of B-17s were lined up on the field and a number of American fighters were just preparing to take off. They received a pasting.

Charlie told his sergeants that evening: "The Japanese struck so adroitly that, in effect, they blasted our U.S. Air Command out of the sky that day." America lost at least half of its B-17 bombers and one fifth of its P-40 fighters.

That first wave of air attacks plunged the island into chaos. Manila was now the next logical target for Japanese bombers. The city contained the USAFFE senior headquarters, occupied by General MacArthur, as well as many supply and military installations in the port area. Nichols and Zamblan Fields were on the outskirts of the city, and sustained low-level strafing the following day.

In Charlie's opinion the Japanese air corps had gained air superiority with that strike, and the fate of the Philippines was determined before a rifle was fired. It is nearly impossible to fight an enemy without an air force to cover and to protect the ground forces.

The success of the Japanese air-strike in the Philippines, just hours after the attack on Pearl Harbor, has sparked controversy to this day. General Brereton, Air Squadron Commander, had repeatedly sought permission before the Philippine attack to launch his B-17s against the Japanese aircraft in Formosa (Taiwan); however he never received a reply from MacArthur's headquarters. MacArthur later insisted that he was unaware of Brereton's request.

The Japanese bombing directly changed Charlie's mindset to that of a soldier at war.

Rounding up Saboteurs

Even before the December 8th bombing, the 808th Military Police had been placed on alert to round up saboteurs. Most saboteurs were civilians who shot flares or used shortwave radios to signal information to the Japanese pilots. Rocket glares were easy to conceal, but a few saboteurs were trained Japanese spies who set explosives to bridges and ammo points.

Charlie's MP unit succeeded in pursuing locals lighting signal and marker flares. Exchanges of gunfire sometimes occurred. One night, he investigated a place along the Pasig River where someone was flashing lights for Japanese planes, directing them to a military target in Manila Bay. Shots were fired and he returned fire. The enemy escaped on foot.

While there were organized teams of saboteurs, the MPs discovered that most were local peasants asked to ignite markers for a few Philippine pesos. Some were caught in the act and turned over to the Philippine Army Department provost marshal or the Philippine Constabulary, who told them to discontinue.

Support from these rural natives would prove essential when war broke out. Two or three pesos went a long way. The influx of Army vehicles over provincial roads, farm paths, and cart tracks also alarmed the populace. In one incident, a village farmer complained that an Army truck had rammed into his fence, killing two chickens and a caraboa (water buffalo). This deprived him of a livelihood. Charlie and his interpreter investigated. He examined the fence, which was two hundred yards off the road and likely not involved. The water buffalo was bruised and limped but was otherwise fine. Charlie suspected the animals were scared by the trucks passing close by and broke free. He developed a good rapport when he told the farmer about his background on a farm in Kansas. After five minutes of a compassionate ear, a settlement of a few American dollars was easily negotiated. It was concluded that the U.S. driver was not at fault, but Charlie did not tell the farmer.

The following week Charlie interviewed an American pilot who flew reconnaissance missions at night over Lingayen Bay. Flares and tracking lights illuminated directions back to targets—in this case, Nichols Air Field. On another night, a truck was set ablaze preceding the bombing of Nichols Field. The portable Pan American beacon station was later found moved to a designated spot and set ablaze for Japanese pilots as a marker.

Trained saboteurs were handled more severely than the recruited peasants. MPs, like other soldiers, saw the danger now as immediate. After the Japanese invasion the tone changed. In the heat of fighting at Layac Junction near the Culo Bridge, one of the militia units caught saboteurs carrying dynamite to blow up the bridge. These saboteurs had Japanese accents, which suggested that they were spies working for the Japanese. They were turned over to the Philippine Department. After questioning, they were shot at the site.

Other nights, Charlie's team homed in on radio stations with locating devices, trying to discover hillside sending locations. Soon over the air they heard the voice of Manila Rose, as she was known to the troops. This alluring female voice introduced a selection of American pop songs, followed by a pretty strong dose of Japanese propaganda. More of this came as the U.S. forces pulled back into a defensive position.

Charlie's request to rejoin a unit as a company line combat officer was delayed in early December. The Command thought he was doing an admirable job pursuing clandestine saboteurs, and this was more important. He was one of the few who knew the leaders of many small villages.

His role increased to even more reconnaissance. He had to locate enemy units by enlisting local help, and then report back to the G-2 intelligence section of his division.

The Japanese Bomb Luzon

The Japanese had good intelligence, and their invasion was well planned and coordinated. One final example: Charlie suspected that his MP station off Dewey Boulevard was under Japanese surveillance from time to time. The day they evacuated Manila, it sustained a direct hit from the air, confirming his suspicions. A major portion of the building was destroyed.

During the defensive build-up, supplies, equipment and vehicles were desperately needed, especially vehicles for troop movement and communications equipment. Out of necessity, the American signal battalion seized the Manila Telephone Company. The military needed it to communicate with field commanders, a process that would remain a constant challenge. Commanders were ordered were to improvise and improvise is what a resourceful officer did! His survival depended on his men's ability to scrounge things. Cars and auto parts were at a premium. On one trip to Manila after a bombing, Charlie noticed a Ford dealership. Without hesitation, he entered the showroom and confiscated a new Ford, taking as many parts as he could carry. He left a note, guaranteeing U.S. payment, redeemable at the conclusion of the war. The next day he turned over the Ford to his motor pool as a new addition to military transportation.

On occasion he drove medical supplies to units or performed a variety of mission requirements as the command saw fit. Any usable equipment and food rations were badly needed. Probably not since the Civil War had a U.S. Army confiscated so much equipment from friendly hands. North of Manila, Charlie found stores of explosives used for blasting in railroad construction, which his unit carted off to be used later.

Military leaders expected additional men and material throughout the coming month of December, 1941. MacArthur repeatedly wired Army Chief of Staff General George Marshall to express outrage about the state of provisions. MacArthur even pressed into action his former executive officer, now brigadier general Dwight Eisenhower, to pressure Washington. "Send supplies to the Philippines!" he urged. Excuses were many, and little, if any, materials came.

The shortage of supplies and weapons caused more harm than the Japanese soldiers toward whipping the U.S. soldiers of the Philippines. Due to the chaos of an evacuation the meager supplies, when found, were poorly utilized. They were either sent haphazardly to Bataan or put on barges to Corregidor. Critical supplies were abandoned. In some instances U.S. forces had to destroy good equipment to prevent the Japanese from obtaining it. On another trip to downtown Manila, Charlie ran into his friend Captain Earl Short assigned to the 31st infantry. Earl was hunting for a wooden crate to secure his regiment's formal Silver Punch Bowl and cup set. He would later become the guardian of these regimental symbols. The night before the Bataan surrender, he escaped to Corregidor with the Punchbowl and cup set, which were later buried, becoming a hidden treasure throughout the war. The two friends did not realize then that they would soon be buddies in a POW prison camp.

It was apparent that the Japanese knew the American-Filipino situation well—our manpower strength and our weakness. The Japanese warlords prepared their invasion forces in the summer of 1941. Not expecting the American-Filipino armies to offer much resistance, they had planned for a fifty-day siege to conquer all of Luzon.

Chapter 4 | MacArthur's Plans, and Initial Probe Landings by the Japanese

Assuming command, General Douglas MacArthur made a hard case for an offensive, rather than defensive war. His plan was to allow the Japanese units land at the beaches, then counterattack, and drive them back to the sea before they could form into a larger force. MacArthur had two capable commanders under him at a corps level to carry out his strategy: General Wainwright and General Parker. Each was given a section of operation—General Wainwright, the I Corps Commander, had the northern sector of Luzon, and General Parker had the south as the II Corps Commander—dividing operational control of the island in half.

A seventy-five-page report titled *The Defense of Luzon and Bataan**, written by Major Charles Underwood in 1947, has been credited by military historians as one of the first eyewitness

---

*Only brief accounts of his report are included herein. The reader is referred to the bibliography for additional information.

MacArthur's Plans

reports of the fighting. Having fought in this sector, Charlie was fortunate to have had frequent discussions with his friend Captain Tom Dooley, who was General Wainwright's aide. He also received the benefit of frequent updates from another friend, Captain Art Christensen, the G-2 intelligence officer.

General Wainwright's Northern Luzon forces consisted of the 11th, 21st, 31st, and 71st Divisions plus the 26th Cavalry Regiment Philippine Scouts (PS). In addition, the 91st Division was attached but contained only two regiments. Together with the Philippine Army Department troops, an element of the 31st, this comprised the USAFFE reserve.

In the days after the 7th of December, intelligence was gathered from the USS Stingray submarine patrolling in the ocean off the north side of Luzon. A Japanese naval force had been spotted, suggesting that forces would likely land at Lingayen Gulf. This is exactly what happened.

On December 10, 1941, at Aparri, a reinforced regiment brigade of Japanese landed on Philippine beaches. The landing was unopposed except for aerial bombardment and strafing. On December 12 the Japanese began a second series of small, probing landings at Vigan, at the northern tip, with a division of troops. Except for a platoon of twenty-six Cavalry scout cars, which were on patrol, the landings were unopposed.

Luzon was now in a state of war against a vastly superior Japanese army. Thus began a ninety-nine day siege. Initially, General Wainwright considered the Aparri and Vigan landings as attempts to divert his troops from the Lingayen Gulf, the expected target of the invasion. Therefore he did not take the bait. He sent only two battalions of U.S. infantry from the 11th Division to Bauang to set up defensive blocking positions to prevent further advance. Wainwright's area of defense was large in scope. With reconnaissance poor, he was constantly on the roadways as troops were shuttled around the island night and day to block Japanese advances.

Meanwhile Charlie was undergoing a real on-the-job training in demolitions, which was normally a combat engineer function. His MPs had earlier found and confiscated TNT at a railroad warehouse near the town of Tarlac. A rail engineer provided rudimentary instructions on setting explosive to remove a tree, a boulder or a mound for track laying—but not for military purposes; that, Charlie would have to learn himself by trial and error.

Charlie did not waste much time. On the early morning of December 10, the MPs put explosives into play for the first time. They planted a charge on a small bridge on a provincial road to block a possible Japanese infantry advance. The blast destroyed the bridge, preventing the enemy from advancing on a U.S. unit. Charlie reflected later on his mission: only a year before he'd been

MacArthur's Plans

a news reporter; now, at age 24, he was planting dynamite and preparing to fight for the lives of himself and his men.

For the American military, preparing for the Japanese invasion was a huge chess game of matching limited manpower to expected points of invasion. There were other distractions for General Wainwright, such as untrained Filipino troops, which were jumpy and unpredictable. For instance, on December 11, the 21st Infantry at one beachhead reported engaging and repulsing an invasion force in a sector of Lingayen Bay. Radio reports, or the lack thereof, kept headquarters commanders up all night. When daylight came, the truth emerged that the untrained Filipino troops had just panicked when they heard a motorized fishing boat, and let loose an entire battery of artillery. They shelled nothing but a poor boat on the water.

Charlie's primary mission now was to assist armed units to keep or clear the main roads for friendly troop movement. He made countless predawn road checks at bridges, posting guards along major highway #3, then reconnoitered along the highway to observe any suspicious activity. Local help was essential. Local Filipinos sent their "all-clear" reports before dawn, by the use of signal lights. Under the veil of early morning light Charlie would arrive at a bridge and ensure that explosives had not been affixed there. Next, he would proceed to nearby hilltops for the best possible view of potential enemy movement as the sun rose. If he observed enemy movement, he'd call in the location, and then get the hell out of that location before he became a target of opportunity.

There were about thirty American press reporters in Manila covering news of the war. MacArthur had given the press unfettered access, including observation of front line fighting. Reporters, from *Life* and *Time* magazines and major newspapers, could go anywhere they desired. At the time of Japanese beach probes, correspondents actually drove vehicles to the far sides of Luzon to watch the fighting, then dashed back to write their stories.

The soldiers appreciated the presence of the journalists who interviewed the troops. The reporters sent messages back home, to the delight of the soldier's families, thus boosting morale. The news also reported the tenuous military situation to the States. Soon a message system was devised at the USAFFE Headquarters level that permitted a short news column of no more than five hundred words to be wired to stateside locations by each correspondent.

One afternoon in early December, Charlie was cornered by several newspaper correspondents he knew. The reporters wanted to go to the front to observe some action. Charlie reluctantly agreed. "I leave at zero six hundred hours (0600), and travel light." He didn't expect them to show.

The next morning at 0600, two correspondents appeared. They worried as they saw Charlie's banged-up and bullet-holed car. The trip was delayed because of fueling, but eventually got on the road. Things were fine until they reached the vicinity of Tarlac. Then, out of the sky, a Japanese Zero swept down and took a first pass. *Ping, Ping, Ping, Ping.* The bullets ricocheted off and around the car. The Zero caused Charlie to swerve off the road into a ditch. The bullets kicked up a lot of dirt on the road. At that point, both correspondents came to the realization that there was indeed a war going on. They sheepishly asked him to turn around citing a need to get the story quickly to their respective papers. Later Charlie got a copy and he remembered only one line: "Intense aerial fight in the west sector of Luzon." His car had sustained another banged-up fender to match the other side. Apparently when swerving off the road, the axle hit hard and bent the frame and the car drove with a shimmy. It was soon discarded for parts.

* * *

Figure 6: Charlie's car after gunfire

MacArthur's Plans

The southern area of Luzon, General Parker's section, suddenly burst into activity on December 12, 1941, with the first landing of Japanese soldiers. Word about the landing arrived by telegram from the local railroad station master at Legaspi, at the southern tip of the island. He bravely remained at his post to insure his telegrams were sent even when the Japanese soldiers advanced up the porch steps of his station. This force, estimated as a reinforced brigade of the Japanese 16th Division with naval escort, landed twenty-five hundred troops virtually unopposed. General Parker sent only token forces from the 41st and the 51st Divisions (PA) to meet the invaders, and a few U.S. fighters harried the enemy naval vessels, but both efforts were ineffective. As in the north, these were considered reconnaissance landings, with the main force to come later. The American strategy in the south was the demolition of bridges in hopes of halting the rapid Japanese advances. Both regions were now on high alert for an island-wide invasion.

Chapter 5 | The Invasion of Luzon

On December 21, 1941, the Japanese went on full scale attack. The first sizable wave of five Japanese divisions hit the beaches in North Luzon. This main invasion occurred at several locations along the Lingayen Gulf and totaled thirty-seven thousand troops.

The Japanese amphibious force made landfall over a large area of the Lingayen Gulf. Due to bad weather and high seas, the landing force drifted. Wind, waves, and currents actually helped push the Japanese safely past the obstacles and defenses established by the 21st and 11th Division interceptors, and they landed with little opposition

In the early morning of December 21, at least sixteen invading ships in the first wave cruised offshore, sitting targets of opportunity—yet, nothing could be done. The U.S. Air Corps was so weak that it could not mount a formidable air attack. U.S. Navy and Army Air Force remnants attacked with what they had, sinking a few ships, annoying others, but not halting the landing force. Soon there were more than fifty ships offloading swarming Japanese troops all across the Lingayen Gulf as far north as Agoo (see Figure 7, invasion chart below.)

The Japanese poured men, tanks and artillery into this area and eventually broke through beach defenses. The 26th Cavalry met the brunt of the invasion force and put up a terrific fight. Their action initially pinned the enemy down until Japanese air support entered the battle with repeated strafing attacks. Once landed, the Japanese could not be contained by U.S.-Filipino forces. The Japanese infantry went on the advance, spearheaded by light tanks, infantry on bicycles, and motorcycles.

Each day the Japanese landed thousands of additional troops in northern Luzon. Territory became a scramble to defend. Large numbers of Japanese pressed hard on all roads, paths and flatland. But the U.S.-Filipino forces stubbornly withdrew in "retro-movement," giving ground only at a high cost. There were many instances of heroic stands by young American field commanders who fled at the last moment, reestablishing defensive positions several miles up the road at key tactical points. Hot on their heels, the Japanese would run into American firepower and be forced to redeploy and clean up the opposition as our side fled once again, across rivers or obstacles. The Japanese then regrouped and took up the chase once more, disregarding all tactics other than a fast pursuit.

Such was the course of the early days of fighting. Charlie's unit worked feverishly to set explosives at key tactical points such as road bridges, while supporting the infantry, until the last possible second—detonating the charge as the last U.S. troops crossed. It was a textbook example of fighting a retrograde action. On occasion, the enemy got too close and nearly overran U.S. forces. At one point during a chase, two Japanese tanks managed to infiltrate the rear of a retreating U.S. column of tanks of the 26th. The American middle had to turn about and unleash heavy fire in order to break off and resume a hasty withdrawal over a bridge before setting it ablaze. Other times, arms and supplies were abandoned as men scrambled to safety before a bridge fell.

Back in division headquarters, reports of casualties became a daily event—yet there was little time to mourn the devastating news of the death of colleagues. Any soldier on Luzon was now in harm's way. All vehicle movement was potentially dangerous and subject to Japanese aerial strafing. Fortunately, the bulk of the Japanese Army focused on pursuing and destroying the 26th Cavalry. This allowed movement for other units. The 26th pinned up the Japanese long enough for other U.S. forces to organize a group to go back and retrieve lost supplies, as well as to prepare a major defense in the rear.

The Invasion of Luzon

Figure 7: Luzon Invasion

As depicted above in Figure 7, the Japanese military arrived from Formosa (Taiwan). Beachhead probing landings occurred first in North Luzon at Aparri on December 10, and at Vigan on December 12, and on the southern Luzon coast near Legaspi. The invasion by 14th Japanese Army on Northern Luzon occurred on December 21 at points along the Lingayen Gulf, and on December 23 by the 16th Japanese Army on three points along Lamon Bay. Calumpit Bridges are located near San Fernando.

Our Adversary—the Japanese Soldier

The Japanese soldier was agile and tenacious. According to division intelligence, he was short, about five feet four inches on average. He was a good wrestler with powerful legs and a solid trunk, and therefore a tough opponent in hand-to-hand combat.

The Japanese infantryman's standard weapon was a bolt-action rifle, superior to our Enfield— it shot farther and would not misfire. Their rifle was about five feet long. It was made of hard wood with a steel barrel and steel butt-plate, and had both the circle sight and raised sight for long-range objects. The bayonet was a fifteen inch blade, and tapered down to a lethal end. It weighed eleven pounds.

The Invasion of Luzon

The Japanese soldier was disciplined harshly by corporal punishment in the form of open-hand slapping by his superiors when he failed to respond appropriately. If he protested by yelling out, he would suffer a beating to make him tougher.

He was indoctrinated by the Bushido Code, which held that it was expected for a soldier to die with honor on the battlefield than to surrender.

The 1940 Japanese soldier was taught that the U.S. Army soldier was amoral and was to be disrespected, that he represented an inferior race and would run and not fight. The few who surrendered to U.S. forces indicated their surprise when we stood our ground and fought hard against them.

The Japanese foot soldier was molded into blind obedience to his leaders. Tactically, in the Burma and China campaigns, he was taught to employ the frontal assault, a charge straight toward the opposing force, requiring enormous self-discipline, but adherence to the Bushido Code stressed that it was an honor to die for one's country. Snipers were the best-trained soldiers; they operated independently and went out alone. They relied on a full backpack containing food for several days, medical supplies in case they were wounded, ropes for rappelling from trees and high objects, and usually a gas mask—in short, a basic survival kit for jungle warfare.

The Japanese officer corps was seen as an elite corps to be revered by the Japanese infantryman. Many Japanese officers were ruthless. Officers exposed to western culture were unpredictable from our point of view—some treated captives humanely, others despised the American soldier.

Fort Stotsenburg and nearby Clark Airfield were hurriedly evacuated in mid-December on erroneous information of immediate overrun, leaving vast provisions virtually intact. With the Japanese tangled up by the 26th Scouts, a group of U.S. forces organized a daring supply pickup, escorted by Charlie's MPs, on the night of December 21. Five trucks were marshaled from their staging area in the dark of night; the drivers were told to use only blackout lights—a slotted amber lens emitting a pale ray of light, which could be seen at a distance of no more than fifteen feet—instead of headlights. MPs manned control points along the road. The U.S. drivers were understandably jumpy—in the back of everyone's mind was the worry that an enemy tank would bolt out and blast the convoy like sitting ducks.

As the small convoy headed for Fort Stotsenburg, Charlie counted the five assigned trucks and began to close in as rear sweep. Then another truck closed in at a fast pace—then another. Instead of five trucks, there were now seven trucks. Charlie rushed alongside. He saw that the last two had airmen drivers. They had apparently decided to join in when they heard of a supply run, and were heading for Clark Airfield to retrieve the weapons and parts off planes. The other truck contained needed medical supplies from Stotsenburg.

The next alarm went off in South Luzon, commanded by General Parker, of Corps II. It was composed of the 41st and 51st Philippine Army Divisions, the 51st Engineer Battalion, 1st Infantry regiment, Philippine Army Division and the 2nd Regiment, Philippine Constabulary. Also in support, but under USAFFE headquarters control, was a battalion of self-propelled 75mm guns, two guns to a battery, and the 194th Battalion of light tanks.

Earlier, on December 19, U.S. forces had learned that the Japanese had landed a battalion of infantry near Spicot. Two companies from the 52nd Infantry were sent to harass and delay the enemy, and were attacked near Timbuyo. The enemy was met by Charlie's close friend, First Lieutenant Matt Dobrinic, who had well prepared his troops. They let loose with every weapon in his company. The enemy was routed and pursued for about a mile until joining up with their larger force, at which time Lieutenant Dobrinic's company suffered significant casualties and was forced to withdraw. They regrouped en route and continued the fight. The Japanese then merged with a larger Japanese landing force at Siain and completely encircled Dobrinic's unit, and it disintegrated. Dobrinic, another officer and a small group of Americans escaped and made their way through Japanese lines. They reported back for duty in Bataan more than a month later. Lieutenant Dobrinic's good fortune continued. Hours before the fall of Bataan, nearly three months later, he once again slipped away in a makeshift boat to Corregidor and took part in that island's final defense.

From the other side of the island, on the evening of December 23, 1941, the second wave of the Japanese invasion occurred in the south, on the beaches of Lamon Bay at three points, beginning at Mauban and ending with their landing unopposed at Siain beachhead farther south, as depicted in Figure 7. Over seven thousand Japanese troops overpowered the U.S.-Filipino defenders. As in north Luzon, the U.S. forces had little air power to oppose the southern invasion. After little resistance, the Japanese 16th Division began the drive north. By the morning of December 24 the Japanese had crossed all roadblocks and opposition and were into Malicbuy. Their next target was Manila.

At this point Luzon citizens began to panic. Charlie, with his small command, had his work cut out for him. Looting occurred in Manila as Filipinos fled to the countryside. An element of the 31st Infantry was now augmented to Charlie's MPs as support, to keep order, clear roads and guard bridges in and around Manila.

On December 24, General Albert Jones took over from General Parker in the south and quickly improvised a system of delaying tactics hoping to stop the Japanese. The next few days saw various hasty positions established, resulting in quick delaying fights before the defenders withdrew to better fortified positions.

As the Japanese followed in pursuit, Jones blew up all but one bridge and controlled their route. On December 27, his sizable American force dug in for a massive counterattack. However, the next day, December 28, USAFFE Headquarters commanded Jones to immediately abort that planned engagement. He was ordered to pull back into a hasty retro-movement to protect Wainwright's exposed right flank, which protected the only escape route to Bataan.

For Charlie, his mission was about to change. He would soon be supporting a total command evacuation to a small peninsula, called Bataan.

Chapter 6 | War Plan Orange— Being Pushed from All Sides

Given the losses sustained by U.S. forces during the first ten days, MacArthur realized his counterattack would not work. Instead, on the night of December 23, he implemented War Plan Orange.

This was a well-planned series of defensive withdrawals all the way past Manila and then into the Bataan Peninsula. Each D-line (defense line), was separated fron the next by a distance that could be covered in one night's march. D-1 was on the beaches. D-2, along the Agno River, was occupied and held on December 24-25 by fighting units of the 11th, 21st, and remnants of the 91st and the 26th Cavalry.

On December 27th, the entire North and South U.S. forces began converging on the junction of Highway 3 and Highway 7. As they converged, traffic was created and soon became magnified by the estimated 20,000 civilian refugees fleeing on the same roads from Manila. With the roads completely clogged, Wainwright's army came to a standstill, and was exposed as an easy target for any Japanese aerial attacks.

Charlie received a flash order through G-2 Major Joe Chabot at Wainwright's headquarters to immediately clear the bottleneck. He arrived on site with his seasoned veterans—the old NCOs, only recently called up, knew the secondary routes and footpaths, and more importantly the mentality of the local Filipinos. By directing the civilians out of the main thoroughfare, they were able to move the military traffic forward toward Bataan within minutes. Charlie felt great pride in his group's success.

General MacArthur's Surprise for Manila

Central to the idea of War Plan Orange was MacArthur's brilliant move to overtly bypass the defense of the capital, Manila. At 1630 hours the afternoon of December 24, Christmas Eve, General MacArthur took to the radio airways and issued his surprise communiqué. "In order to spare lives and the city from both air and ground attack, Manila would be considered an 'open city,' as had been done in the cases of Paris, Brussels and Rome in Europe," he said. He would bypass it as a military defense position, averting civilian casualties. MacArthur, fully aware of his limited army, really had no choice, and declared that Manila was not a military target.

General Homma ordered a pause in action and sought further guidance from Tokyo. For two days tanks and military might formed up just outside Manila awaiting further orders.

While there was a pause in action, Charlie sent home his last message of that year. He said in closing: "With the Trust in God and a steady trigger finger, everything will come out fine for me and the U.S."

After a three-day pause, the Japanese High Command decided to ignore the MacArthur communiqué. Bombing resumed over Manila and the Japanese army stormed into the city, unopposed. That action so incensed the Filipinos that any hope of gaining support for the Japanese reign was forever lost.

Disfavor mounted for Homma in Tokyo. His actions were not praised by Prime Minister Tojo, who began from this point to disfavor General Homma. Against MacArthur, General Homma had met his master in terms of the politics of the art of war. MacArthur, who seldom failed to use the power of words, decried the attack on Manila as "uncivilized." He pointed out that even the Nazi German Army had spared Paris. The negative reaction gnawed at Homma and brought embarrassment to his country—probably one of the factors that would cost Homma his career before spring ended.

Perhaps due to the pause, the extra time allowed General Wainwright to complete his mission. By the early-morning hours of January 1, 1942, all American-Filipino units of I and II Corps had successfully made their escape across the Calumpit Bridges, and into the Bataan Peninsula—quite a military feat. Charlie's MPs assisted other armed units in keeping the main road passable, then each bridge crossed was immediately blown up. Troops were not permitted to stop, each stalled vehicle was pushed off the road as there was not time for repairs, and locals were held in check. Charlie considered his contribution to this effort, meager.

On January 5 and 6, the 31st Infantry was positioned on one side of the main road with the 26th Cavalry. There were also untested units on the line that had not experienced hostile fire. They failed to take things seriously, did not dig in and seemed to have doubts regarding the advancing Japanese. So unreal was their attitude that Filipino boys went up and down their sector selling San Miguel beer from a tub for a couple pesos like a jamboree. Then reality struck. On the 6th of January, the Japanese artillery opened up and peppered the entire area. Those units were the first to flee.

Charlie's good friend Captain John Pray of G Company 31st Infantry held his position despite the heavy and repeated bombardment. He continued to provide cover for the remaining units. Pray crawled from foxhole to foxhole to steady the nerves of his men, who thought they were certainly goners. In the thick smoke, he was more than once reported dead. He told Charlie later that the impulse to bolt and run was great; then for a moment he caught sight of another surreal scene, a small redstart bird chirping away in a tree while artillery exploded around him. If a little red bird could take it, so could he, Pray decided; he miraculously survived with most of his men.

Hours later, big Captain Gene Conrad, Company B of the 31st fought up on his flank. Seeing an opening and without orders, Conrad led a counterattack and saved the day by repulsing the oncoming Japanese infantry. Gene Conrad's actions signified the toughness of our fighting force. "This would be no cakewalk for the oncoming Japanese army," as Charlie later noted. The U.S.-Filipino force was still a formidable army.

Chapter 7 | The Siege of Bataan

Bataan is twenty-five miles long and twenty miles wide. Bataan of 1942 was a remote, underdeveloped province consisting of jungles and swamps and inhabited by monkeys, wild boars, snakes, spiders and worst of all mosquitos. Only a few towns dotted the coastline. Highway 7 entered the peninsula at the north end. The main paved road, Highway 110, followed the east coast to Mariveles and then proceeded up the west coast. The old cobblestone Bagac-Pilar Road cut through the valley between two mountain ranges. The security of Bataan lay in control of these three main roads.

A network of trails had been cut in the interior, largely by lumber companies in the 1930s, but workers soon abandoned the area due to an insidious outbreak of malaria, caused by mosquitoes. In 1942 these became military paths of travel and were just large enough to be used by vehicles.

To defend Bataan, on January 7, 1942, the U.S.-Filipino Army established a long defensive line that cut across the entire peninsula from Mauban West to Abucay (Abucay-Mauban Line, see figure 8). The Abucay-Mauban line, as it was called, had in the middle of it a 4,300-foot extinct volcano, Mount Natib, which broke up the U.S.-Filipino line integrity. Control of Mount Natib, the highest strategic point, was absolutely vital for U.S. artillery observers to see enemy movement. If the enemy got this position, the Japanese could look down the throats of American forces, making them easy targets. Contact between I Corps and II Corps was never fully made; each side ran its defenses from the coast to the slopes of Mount Natib without ensuring contact, and that gap later became a fatal flaw in our overall defense.

I Corps, with responsibility for the west sector of Bataan, consisted of about twenty-two thousand men, and was first commanded by General Wainwright. The I Corps included chiefly the 1st, 31st, 71st, and 91st Divisions and the 26th Cavalry. The 31st (US) and 45th (PS) regiments and the tanks were still under MacArthur's control (USAFFE).

Corps II was on the east sector under General A.M. Jones, with twenty-five thousand troops. It was made up of essentially the 11th, 21st, 41st, 43rd, and 51st Divisions and the 57th Infantry Regiment Philippines Scouts, and the 4th Philippine Constabulary Regiment defended the bottom southern end of Bataan as shown in Figure 8 below.

Upon arrival on Bataan, Charlie received a message from General A.M. Jones, of II Corps, requesting that he be assigned to "advise" the 4th Constabulary. His reaction to that notice both pleased and concerned him. He would have a commander status but the 4th Filipino Regiment had just been called up.

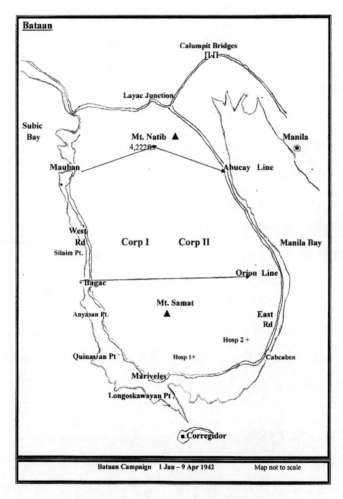

Figure 8: Map of Bataan Positions

Charlie's new role in the 4th Filipino Regiment

On January 7, 1942, as U.S.–Filipino forces moved into our final defense. The Constabulary units were under the overall command of Philippine Major General Guillermo Francisco. The 4th mobilized, was the very last battalion of the Philippine campaign to do so, only days before Charlie arrived, and was the weakest.

The 4th Constabulary knew nothing about combat tactics. In fact, one friend of Charlie's referred to his unit as the "left-overs—overweight clerks," a description which Charlie never agreed with (but they *were* untrained.) He found them eager to learn. The regiment was formed by combining men from various locations on Luzon, and rounded up the unused administrative personnel. This haphazard composition made training for warfare a much needed, immediate concern. These factors left Charlie, no doubt, with a formidable task as their commander.

His unit was half its intended size of three line companies and one machine-gun company. For heavy weapons, each company had one Browning automatic rifle, four or five .30-caliber machine guns left over from WWI, and the old three-inch mortars that had an estimated seventy percent dud rate! Many of his troops had never fired a rifle, many had never been in the field.

Charlie's regiment had two mission requirements: first, to defend the lower east coast between Mariveles and Cabcaben against hostile beachhead landings. And second, to reinforce other units as needed. When called by higher headquarters, they had to prepare for movement on a thirty-minute notice.

First, Charlie directed his troops to dig defensive fortifications along a stretch of beach at the southern and eastern tip of Bataan, from Mariveles and Cabcaben. Then Charlie trained the men in the absolute basics: how to fire a weapon and marksmanship. Few had actually "zeroed" their rifle, aligning the sight to target. He had a week to accomplish this and prepare them to fight like an army.

There were a lot of problems, the greatest being basic communication. They did not understand any tactical terms, or even agreement of what "yes" meant. For instance, most nodded "yes" as a polite greeting out of respect, but with little intent of compliance. Charlie found that the Filipino said "yes" to everything just because they wanted to please the one in charge. In the field, the hand signals were somewhat helpful; interpreters more so. Only one of his companies had any understanding of the principles of defensive warfare, thanks to training by the U.S.

forces and chiefly because of a feisty, stout Filipino nicknamed Hacki because of the way he wielded a razor-sharp machete. He was trained and resourceful, and rose from the ranks to be a capable unit leader. Later, if a map was needed, he would somehow get one, often off a dead Japanese soldier.

On Charlie's first night of defense his men were nervous, keyed up by an alert of a possible landing. Suddenly one squad began firing, spooked by a strange noise out on the water; the whole platoon discharged their weapons before he could get them under control. Charlie was aghast. They were firing at wooden debris crashing against rocks. The "buddy system" of two men per foxhole had not worked well. The men were too nervous.

Charlie summoned his leaders and simplified their defensive strategy. He replaced two-man teams with three-man or even four-man teams for each position. As a small group, they found courage in numbers. That actually beefed up defenses because the men became more disciplined and it curbed the impulse to dash to the rear, but it shortened their defensive line.

Later, as jungle warriors, they performed acceptably on small reconnaissance patrols and were good scouts, blending well into jungle camouflage. As food became scarce, they organized a fishing "fleet"; catches were few, yet they caught enough to sustain a man's diet for a while.

In terms of warfare tactics, Charlie and other commanders would soon learn that deployment of soldiers was difficult in a jungle, or any location on Bataan. Terrain was dense, and roads were constantly clogged with vehicles, carts, and hordes of fleeing civilians. U.S. engineers hastily constructed more roads, but that only made matters worse, opening routes for civilians who fled to Bataan seeking protection from the Japanese. An estimated twenty thousand locals were fed and cared for by the U.S. Military during the defense of Bataan.

The Abucay-Mauban line is attacked and falls to the enemy.

On January 9, 1942, in the north sector of Bataan, Japanese forces, led by Lieutenant General Susumu Morioka, assaulted the eastern flank of the Abucay-Mauban Line. They were repulsed by the 91st Division and 57th. At one point against the 57th position, the Japanese were spotted coming down the east road in close column. That was all the Americans needed; the U.S. artillery blasted them to bits. Two days later, after regrouping, the Japanese tried again.

Attempting to penetrate the lines in a night attack, the Japanese drove caraboas (water buffalos) ahead of their attack to detonate the mines that had been planted. The poor animals' bellows and moans could be heard throughout the night.

On January 11, the 3rd Battalion 57th was attacked in force. It held and cleared out the enemy by tapping its reserve company of fighters. At 0430 on January 12, the Japanese attacked again across the east front, hitting the sector's obstacles with great fury. Although the enemy suffered great losses, with hundreds left hanging on barbed wire, the Japanese managed to penetrate the Abucay-Mauban line into U.S.-Filipino positions. This created a bulge, but not a break in the defensive line. Two battalions of the 21st (PA) Division counterattacked and had limited success repairing the defensive line. The nights of January 14 and 16 saw repeated Japanese assaults on the defensive Abucay-Mauban Line held by the 51st and 42nd.

On January 19, 1942, a near-fatal blow was struck when the Japanese 9th Infantry cleverly penetrated U.S. defenses by scaling the slopes of Mount Natib. To the American's astonishment, they had now outflanked the U.S.-Filipino defenders. The Abucay-Mauban Line could no long serve as a defensive battle line and was abandoned on January 22, 1942. Winning precious terrain, the Japanese victory pushed the Americans back. At best, it can be said that the U.S. strategy delayed the Japanese advance, creating the necessary time needed for expected supplies to arrive from the States.

Battle of the Pockets, Battle of the Points—Americans' Last Success

The U.S.-Filipino force drew back in a retro movement to the next defensive line—the Orion-Bagac Line. The Japanese Army kept up the pressure during the withdrawal, mounting a strong penetration along the west coast and cliffs. At first U.S. intelligence underestimated the force of their advance; these landings at three areas were thought to contain only a small force. But late January through mid-February of 1942 saw a period of very bloody fighting against several thousand Japanese troops.

On January 24, Charlie received an order to pack up and move elements of his command to the West Road in the vicinity of Quinauan Point. His deployment supported the 2nd Constabulary, engaged there with an estimated fifty Japanese soldiers who had scaled the cliffs of the promontory infiltrating into that sector.

Arriving by bus, Charlie's unit had barely formed up in a rear assembly area when bullets flew overhead. Little could be made out through the thick undergrowth of the heavily forested terrain. Pinned down initially, Charlie tried in vain to raise his relief, the 2nd Constabulary, by radio for an update, then higher command for any current information on the enemy strength. The sound of gunfire, coming from his immediate north, allowed him to locate the 2nd Constabulary sector. He followed the action.

His troops moved forward but stayed low and dispersed. Suddenly Japanese snipers in the trees fired, and bullets ricocheted wildly around them. Charlie ordered his men into a staggered battle line and urged them to crawl forward toward the firing. His men hesitated; then they begin firing blindly and, to his surprise, ran back to his rear, took up positions, and fired again, and ran to the rear again! This was Charlie's introduction to his men in action and their style of fighting. This battle was called the Battle of the Pockets. It was the enemy's attempt to take the West Road.

By late afternoon his unit had not advanced at all, but he had learned to direct his men by assuming a forward position (not ordering from a rear position, which normally affords a wider view of the situation). When he led, they would follow him. With this accommodation, he managed to control the unit.

By day's end his unit had only advanced about thirty yards forward in a very tough fight. The second and third day was similar but his unit's integrity was maintained.

Figure 9: Cliffs of Quinaun Point

Photo compliments of Johnny Olson

The Siege of Bataan

In a later report, Charlie described how the Battle of the Pockets "involved fighting yard by yard, hole by hole, against a very stubborn, well-trained Japanese force." It took more than several days to surround the Japanese unit. Strategically, once surrounded, their actions were pointless. The Americans offered lenient surrender terms; the Japanese only attempted to break out through American-Filipino lines and failed. Charlie's unit sealed one flank to prevent any such breakout. Obeying instructions on leaflets dropped by Japanese planes in the closing days of the battle, some of the trapped Japanese attempted to assemble rafts, most swam to the north in an attempt to escape. A large number of swimmers drowned.

Ultimately, a platoon of U.S. tanks from the 3rd Battalion 45th Infantry went into the terrain by a series of coordinated tank-infantry attacks. "Although only two tanks at a time could be deployed in this rugged terrain, this was one of the few occasions where an infantry-tank team worked well together," Charlie later wrote. American tanks gave overhead protection to the infantry from the Japanese snipers firing from trees and from landmines buried in the ground. "The tanks not only furnished cover for the infantrymen walking along with them, but they also were able to blast at caves and fire their machine guns into the holes," Charlie reported. Their deaths seemed pointless to the Americans, but they chose to follow their Bushido Code, death with honor

In a second area, more inland, the Japanese had constructed trenches and tunnels. This action was called the "upper pockets," but the outcome for the American-Filipino side proved similar. They were aided by volunteers from the Igorote Tribe of the 11th Division, who rode atop buttoned-down U.S. tanks which inflicted many enemy casualties. They fired down into the trenches as the tanks rolled over them. Again, few Japanese surrendered; most fought to their death.

On January 23rd, the Japanese 20th Infantry struck the southwest coast again. An ad hoc force including men from the Air Corps as infantry, the 21st, 34th, 71st, 803rd and the Constabulary Units contained the beachhead landing at Lapay-Longoskawayan Points. Here Charlie's friend, famed flyer Captain Ed Dyess traded his wings for an infantry rifle and did more than a respectable job in pinning the enemy down.

In these coastal engagements, the American Sector Commander, General McBride, took pride in his unseasoned ad hoc forces. They could at least halt the enemy's advance, allowing time to bring up better-trained regulars for the kill.

The last battle in the area was at Anyasan-Silaiin Points. Just north, a large Japanese landing of the 20th Infantry occurred in late January. American intelligence was good, since enemy plans had been discovered earlier on the body of a dead Japanese captain. Japanese landing barges were subjected to aerial and

The Siege of Bataan

naval attacks. The Japanese troops were met on the beaches by the 45th, the 57th, the 1st and 2nd Constabulary Battalions, artillery, and the 192nd Tank Battalion. Amid fierce fighting, all the Japanese were repulsed by February 13, 1942.

After this beating, Japanese General Homma pulled back his weary army to the outskirts of Manila. Since January 9, the Japanese had suffered staggering losses of seven thousand battle casualties, with another ten thousand men dying of disease; half of Homma's remaining troops were ill with malaria. The American-Filipino forces reported far fewer casualties. Charlie's unit was bused back to his east position.

Only fifty Japanese soldiers were taken prisoner in these battles. Except for a handful captured by II Corps, these were the only prisoners taken so far by the Bataan force. Interrogation of these prisoners revealed that the Japanese soldiers faced similar problems as our men; they were short on rations and water, sweltered in the jungle heat, and were plagued by bouts of dysentery and malaria. Like the American soldiers, most just wanted to go home.

The Battle of the Pockets and the Battle of the Points represented the first time a large division of the Japanese army had been defeated by troops of Philippine soldiers, supported by U.S. soldiers in the Bataan conflict. The Japanese were in near disarray, their morale was low. Later, General Homma said that a major attack on his units then would have put an end to his invasion force, confirming his eroding state of readiness.

The defense-line strategy for the U.S. stubbornly continued. Lost in this strategy was the element of surprise. The Japanese still had the U.S.-Filipino Army pinned down. In telegrams to Washington, U.S. generals pleaded with leaders in Washington for critical reinforcements. They heard promises, but nobody came. Meanwhile, the Japanese now had the time to plan against a one-dimensional and weakening force.

There was a break in fighting, and both sides regrouped. Japanese General Homma used his time wisely. He sent his commanders out to evaluate the tactics of past mistakes—carefully studying the abandoned American defenses on Abucay-Mauban Line. The Japanese saw the error of solely frontal attacks against built-up positions. In short, Homma developed a new strategy for the next phase. It relied heavily on a campaign of total bombardment of a sector, followed by a surgical deployment of both frontal and additional flanking assault forces. It was to work well.

Throughout it all, the combined U.S.-Filipino forces felt they could defeat the Japanese and morale was still high. "Fresh troops are on their way," they were told. "Hold on a bit longer, boys." But there was no resupply and the wait only weakened the American–Filipino force.

The Siege of Bataan

During the pause in fighting each night, which occurred about an hour before sunset as the light began fading, throughout Bataan small U.S.-Filipino recon patrols were sent forward of lines, in an attempt to gain supplies off bodies and to gain a fix on the exact location of the enemy. For example, if a recon patrol discovered Japanese wearing clean uniforms that likely meant the arrival of new reinforcements. The patrols had to be quick before the Japanese artillery began shelling U.S. lines shortly after darkness. Sometimes the enemy's location could be quickly found by merely finding the landline "como" wire and then tracing the wire back to a Japanese outpost. U.S. wire was thin and black; the Japanese used a thicker rusty-orange line.

One evening in mid-February, a recon squad consisting of Charlie, Hacki, and eight others explored a less familiar area of their sector. An artillery shell burst about two hundred yards away. Catching sight of a foxhole, Charlie immediately crawled into it, where he discovered two Japanese bodies lying face-down. Frantically, he searched for maps and food—then froze when he heard Japanese voices about fifty yards off. He evaded capture by covering himself with the bodies of the dead Japanese soldiers.

Charlie looked around for the quickest direction of retreat, his thoughts in turmoil. The situation was precarious. He quickly slid out and performed "the fastest combat crawl" he'd ever done back to the friendly control point. Charlie noted the location. All his major attack on his units then would have put an end to his invasion force, confirming his eroding state of readiness.

The defense-line strategy for the U.S. stubbornly continued. Lost in this strategy was the element of surprise. The Japanese still had the U.S.-Filipino Army pinned down. In telegrams to Washington, U.S. generals pleaded with leaders in Washington for critical reinforcements. They heard promises, but nobody came. Meanwhile, the Japanese now had the time to plan against a one-dimensional and weakening force.

There was a break in fighting, and both sides regrouped. Japanese General Homma used his time wisely. He sent his commanders out to evaluate the tactics of past mistakes—carefully studying the abandoned American defenses on Abucay-Mauban Line. The Japanese saw the error of solely frontal attacks against built-up positions. In short, Homma developed a new strategy for the next phase. It relied heavily on a campaign of total bombardment of a sector, followed by a surgical deployment of both frontal and additional flanking assault forces. It was to work well.

Throughout it all, the combined U.S.-Filipino forces felt they could defeat the Japanese and morale was still high. "Fresh troops are on their way," they were told. "Hold on a bit longer, boys." But there was no resupply and the wait only weakened the American–Filipino force.

The Siege of Bataan

During the pause in fighting each night, which occurred about an hour before sunset as the light began fading, throughout Bataan small U.S.-Filipino recon patrols were sent forward of lines, in an attempt to gain supplies off bodies and to gain a fix on the exact location of the enemy. For example, if a recon patrol discovered Japanese wearing clean uniforms that likely meant the arrival of new reinforcements. The patrols had to be quick before the Japanese artillery began shelling U.S. lines shortly after darkness. Sometimes the enemy's location could be quickly found by merely finding the landline "como" wire and then tracing the wire back to a Japanese outpost. U.S. wire was thin and black; the Japanese used a thicker rusty-orange line.

One evening in mid-February, a recon squad consisting of Charlie, Hacki, and eight others explored a less familiar area of their sector. An artillery shell burst about two hundred yards away. Catching sight of a foxhole, Charlie immediately crawled into it, where he discovered two Japanese bodies lying face-down. Frantically, he searched for maps and food—then froze when he heard Japanese voices about fifty yards off. He evaded capture by covering himself with the bodies of the dead Japanese soldiers.

Charlie looked around for the quickest direction of retreat, his thoughts in turmoil. The situation was precarious. He quickly slid out and performed "the fastest combat crawl" he'd ever done back to the friendly control point. Charlie noted the location. All his men were accounted for. "Close call!" he thought. Back at base camp, he immediately called in a division artillery strike on the Japanese unit they had just encountered.

Hacki then noticed that blood was dripping down Charlie's right leg over his boot. A medic was called up. Then, at the field hospital, doctors extracted a two-inch piece of shrapnel from his leg just above the knee. Charlie limped for a week, and then recovered fully; a scar remained the rest of his life.

Charlie lost contact with Hacki the first week in April under intense bombardment in the last days of the siege. A POW buddy told him that Hacki had escaped by blending in with the Filipino population, and later joined the guerrilla fighters.

On March 11th, 1942 General MacArthur was ordered to evacuate out of the Philippines by President Franklin Roosevelt. MacArthur's departure further sank the morale of the remaining troops. Charlie, like many others, was stunned to hear this news and felt abandoned. It was as if the star quarterback had been pulled from a championship game.

The command explained MacArthur's evacuation to the American soldiers as a political move on his part to drum up more stateside support. In his departing speech, MacArthur declared, "I shall return!" and to his credit he never forgot his lost command. MacArthur handed over command to General Wainwright. In turn, General Edward King was selected to assume Wainwright's old command, I Corps.

By March 15, 1942, the estimate of combat-ready troops sank to a low of around 25 percent of the original forces. Each day it dropped due to starvation, illness and causalities. Small-arms ammunition was plentiful, even to the end, but artillery munitions were scarce. The U.S. artillery fire was rationed to only missions of extreme necessity. Food was rationed to 1.6 ounces of salmon with 4 ounces of rice per man, per day.

For the next three-and-a-half years, there were two enemies to fight: first, the Japanese Army and, secondly, hunger and starvation.

Chapter 8 | The Japanese Breakthrough and the Fall of Bataan

While severe problems existed every day, the Americans continued a valiant defense, conceding nothing. In Tokyo, the Japanese war minister became displeased at the slowness of Homma's progress. Victory was not coming quickly—not within the expected fifty days—and not without severe losses. He considered removing General Homma.

Homma pleaded with Imperial Headquarters for reinforcements. From mid-March through early April the Japanese received replacements from Japan to fill out their 16th Division and 65th Brigade and 4th Division; more than twenty-two thousand fresh troops were added, supported by more naval ships and better artillery, aerial spotting balloons, and radios. In short, Homma got everything he wanted to renew the siege of Bataan.

With fresh Japanese troops, equipment, and complete air superiority there was little doubt of what was to come. The Japanese smelled victory.

The Japanese Breakthrough and the Fall of Bataan

On April 1, 1942, aerial bombardment of American rear areas began, followed by incessant air strikes across the Orion-Bagac defensive line positions. On April 2, 1942, Japanese generals began a massive artillery bombardment on the 41st and 21st divisions in sector D. Miles of obstacles—barbed wire, trenches and barriers—were taken out in the first hour as shells hailed down with unrelenting ferocity. The thunderous bombardment continued nonstop until the afternoon. Counter-battery fire from the American-Filipino side was sporadic in return. Japanese Zeros circled the battlefield and swept down on anything that moved on the American-Filipino side. A heavy infantry attack, supported by light tanks, charged the left front along the entire 41st Division line. The 42nd and 43rd Regiments were routed by the tremendous tank charge.

The Japanese 65th Brigade and 4th Division spearheaded the main attack on II Corps. At key points along the defensive line, American and Filipino defenders crumbled and were driven back by Japanese tanks and infantry. Tanks rolled over living and dead. Only the 41st withdrew in some order. Simultaneously the 21st Division was heavily attacked and somehow held. So began the brutal pace of the next three days—Good Friday to Easter Sunday, 1942.

The Philippine Army troops of the 42nd and 43rd, and in part the 41st, abandoned their arms and equipment, and fled the battlefield. The 57th (PS) and the 31st Infantry Regiments were pinpointed by

Japanese observation planes. Incendiary bombing was let loose on their sector, which was in dry cogon grass, setting the entire section ablaze, and the 42nd withdrew because of the intense heat.

On the evening of April 7, the 4th Constabulary, located in the rear, received a flash order from General King to move out with other reserve units and join up in a new combat line at Lamoa River.

However, General Clifford Bluemel, the area service commander, amended the order. He needed Charlie and his unit to stay and defend the East Road. Thus, the 4th was split in half.

The detachment that moved rushed up without benefit of reconnaissance and crossed the Lamoa River. A well-armed Japanese force laid waiting. The Japanese inflicted a high kill rate, killing almost all of the advance party, many of whom were Charlie's friends. The few survivors withdrew in confusion and fled south, not to be heard from again until the end of hostilities.

The remaining company under Charlie began fortifying near the Alangan River near the East Road. Their mission now was to halt the Japanese drive toward Mariveles. On the right was Colonel Irwin's 31st (PA) Infantry line, reinforced by the 2nd Engineer Battalion. Neither group had been fed in two days and were exhausted.

The Japanese Breakthrough and the Fall of Bataan

Shortly after dawn they were spotted by Japanese observation planes. Within minutes the first swarm of Japanese fighters strafed and bombed their positions, sending men scrambling for cover. When it seemed to be over, most of the men resumed their positions—only to have a second swarm return with more planes. This time, the bombardment was lethal, killing men and blowing up supplies. Shrapnel zinged over Charlie's head, bomb blast made his ears throb. The men dove for cover into the nearby woods.

When the second wave of planes disappeared, fewer men reformed—many had fled. With much effort, the officers marshaled the remaining men back into line, only to be attacked a third time minutes later. This time when the men broke to the trees, they would not return. At this point they were sitting ducks with no real weapons to mount any defense. The three Japanese air strikes had wounded over eighty, killed at least ten, and disoriented the group. Many soldiers were in a state of shock. The position was abandoned.

The will to fight was gone. Troops had not eaten in two days; weak, ill, and gaunt, their uniforms as tattered as their morale, they did not have the strength to even carry their heavy weapons forward. The morale was not helped by the sight of the Philippine Army fleeing through their defenses the other way.

Charlie's men asked, "Where were the reinforcements, promised by MacArthur and Roosevelt? Where were any rations?" At that point they needed food, medicine, munitions and fresh troops. And Charlie had no answers for his men. They were a starving, dispirited and forsaken army, yet they had held off the Japanese for more than ninety days.

In the last two days of the defense of Bataan, the American-Filipino defense progressively disintegrated and collapsed. Refugees and fleeing Philippine troops clogged all roads, making it impossible to move units up from reserve. At this point, both officers and men were past the point of exhaustion. Remnants of units tried to provide cover fire as others evacuated in the hope of regrouping later. Some surrendered to the Japanese in small groups. Meanwhile, any troop movement drew air attack raids from the Japanese planes.

General Bluemel informed the overall field commander General King that most units had now ceased to exist as such, and could not be expected to offer any means of organized resistance. All that was left were remnants of the 57th (PS) and 31st (US) Infantry Regiments, 26th (PS) Regiment and the 14th (PS) Engineer Battalion. Small parties from the previous right flank had formed into "combat teams" in a makeshift line on the right at about 2100 hours on April 8, with fewer than fifteen hundred men.

The Japanese Breakthrough and the Fall of Bataan

General Bluemel was told to hold the terrain, while a white flag would be sent up for surrender. That night nurses in field hospitals #1 and #2 were evacuated to Corregidor by open boats. Prior to surrender, the remaining U.S. ammunition was exploded. Radios were smashed, vehicles demolished, and guns made inoperative. Only two days issue of one-third rations remained when the U.S. forces surrendered.

April 9, 1942, General King decided to surrender in order to save lives. He surrendered to Colonel Nakayama, the highest Japanese leader in his area who was on the staff of the overall commander, General Homma. It was the largest surrender of American soldiers to date. Fighting ceased temporarily. Homma, however, was perturbed that the surrender only included the Bataan command and not the troops on Corregidor.

Following orders of their commander, Charlie's unit—now no more than a large platoon—laid weapons down and marched to an assembly area in Mariveles, on April 9.

Part III

The Death March and O'Donnell
and Cabanatuan Camp #1 Prison Camps

Chapter 9 | The Death March

"We were ordered to surrender by our commander General King. I was embittered about that decision for the rest of the war."
—Interview with Colonel (ret) Charlie Underwood, 2004.

After Charlie and his men had disposed of their weapons, he went to a designated area with other Americans. The soldiers were then directed to sit on the grass and wait. Japanese soldiers patrolled around them. The Americans were left in the hot sun for hours without food or water. To his right was another small American–Filipino group.

In the afternoon a Japanese officer began to inspect that group. Japanese soldiers removed articles of money, jewelry, newspapers, and identification. Any American soldier found with Japanese articles or money was struck in the back of the head with a rifle stock.

The Death March

Figure 10: Captain Underwood was officially reported captured by the Japanese Army eight months after capture, by telegram as indicated above on 11 December 1942.

Charlie whispered to others around him to get rid of watches, money, jewelry, everything. Within minutes, a Japanese captain stood in front of him. An interpreter introduced the officer in a formal manner; the group was called to attention. The Japanese officer grinned at Charlie as the interpreter prepared to inspect and look for any "forbidden articles". Any man found with such articles would be suitably punished—and any man found with a weapon would be executed.

The shakedown began; Charlie was patted down first and then the shakedown began with the first line of troops. Three or four of his soldiers were searched; nothing was found and the search stopped. And then from out of nowhere, Charlie felt a swift blow to his neck—the Japanese officer had struck him with a bamboo stick. The pain stung but he did not buckle. He remained stoic. Charlie knew that if he caused any incident, a severe beating would follow. The Japanese officer stared at him. Leaning forward, he addressed Charlie in perfect English: "You will not live to see the sun set if you give one more order to your men. *We* do that now! You have no rank anymore. You are prisoners. Get into the line." Charlie did so promptly. Introduction over, the Japanese officer snapped to and walked off to the next group.

It would not be the last time Charlie was hit. This was only a harbinger of rough handling yet to come. His group was allowed to keep their canteens, mess gear and a few clothes articles in a bag.

The Death March

The prisoners moved out and in minutes merged with another group. There Charlie saw the friendly faces of two of his pals—Tex and Walt—but acknowledged nothing for fear of reprisal.

Next, men were sorted into columns of two, the American soldiers on the left side of the road, and the Filipinos on the right side of the road. They began their march in two columns. Given no water or food, the waves of men surged forward. Charlie was between Tex and Walt and they remained together throughout the long march.

The march began at a walking pace. After 15 minutes it quickened to a double-time run. Some men fell out and were sent to the rear. Japanese guards alongside threatened and menaced. One heavy Japanese sergeant came up to Charlie yelling and threatening with his weapon. "You not tough," he scolded in broken English. "You bad Americans!" he taunted. "I look you later, we then see." Charlie steadfastly kept his eyes straight and ignored the name calling.

It was a hot, dry day and dust kicked up beneath their feet as they marched; breathing became difficult. The need for water was great. The Filipino to his right in the other column fell back and immediately was jabbed by a sharp bayonet. Charlie was helpless to do anything. *Keep marching*, he thought, and the man somehow did.

If a soldier fell out, a guard would jab once with a bayonet or use the butt end of his rifle. The man was expected to resume the march, bleeding. If he failed to, he would be dispatched with no remorse. Any vacant space left in the line remained only for seconds as another POW would be prodded forward to fill it.

Soon into the march, a few of the sick complained of the conditions, and they were told to fall back to the rear. *That was odd*, Charlie thought. About eight minutes later, he was startled by the sounds of gunfire coming from the rear; they were shot. Charlie got the message.

Thus began the four-day 100 kilometer march of horror and brutality against American and Filipino POWs.

The only reprieve from the intolerable conditions came from locals—Filipino farmers, women and children who ran ahead to throw balls of rice or leave a jug of water. When a Japanese guard saw this, he'd shoot at them and kick the jug over..

The first day there was only one short stop by a filthy water ditch, and men lapped up water—contaminated water—like wild dogs. That night, the men were herded into barbed-wire pens without a toilet and slept leaning against one another as best they could. Few slept in these conditions. The next morning they were abruptly woken, and many struggled to just get up. Charlie and

The Death March

Tex, who were strong by nature, rose quickly to get their comrades up and going. Charlie tried to help others any way he could—reasoning, ordering, and then cajoling. He successfully cajoled a few of them to honorably represent America, and about a dozen stood up. His friend Walt was hobbling on open blisters, but would not quit. Men ripped up clothing to make bandages. Their first meal of that day was a ball of rice when they came to a village called Balanga.

The second night all were herded into pens and the men collapsed in pain. They tried to get rest amid the moans, tried to ignore the ever-present filth and human waste. Some died overnight. Those who failed to rise in the morning, after one warning, were used like pin cushions for Japanese bayonets. One example: to Charlie's horror, a Japanese officer went up and with the flat side of his sword smacked at a wounded Filipino; when he refused to rise, the next swing beheaded the prisoner.

The third day, as the bedraggled column passed a crossroads before the village of Orani, Japanese tanks were parked on the side of the road. Without warning, a tank suddenly darted out into the front of the column, crushing four prisoners in its way. Charlie could hardly believe what he had witnessed and never got that scene out of his mind.

Charlie fought off the sense of utter despair. By the third day the physical drain on all was becoming dire. But they somehow got up in the morning and began to move. It was sweltering hot by midday. Then, ahead of him, Tex Evans suddenly collapsed. Quickly, Charlie shook Tex. If Tex was not up in seconds, he would be bayoneted. A guard jumped right on top of him and leveled his rifle at Charlie's chest. Charlie glanced downward expecting to be shot but then saw Tex's boot; the heel had come ajar, and immediately exclaiming, "Heel broke, heel broke," he pointed to Tex's boot, shaking it and his buddy in the attempt to revive him. "He's okay, he's okay!"

The guard looked at the broken heel and then laughed. He thought it was funny! After several shakes Tex revived. Having rested for a couple of minutes, both were up and back in the column, dragging onward. "Keep moving," he thought, "just keep moving." "Don't let these bastards get the best of you," he told Tex.

The prisoners, now pushed far beyond the point of exhaustion and pain, found out that even when you have nothing left, you still find you have more inside you. Charlie became crazy for some liquid or water to drink. His mind wandered back to childhood memories of working on the farm. He was eight or nine years old, plowing the fields with his brother; it was a day-long toil and he was hard-pressed to keep up with his older brother. He became exhausted, yet finished the 15 hour day, and received his brother's praise.

The Death March

By the afternoon of the fourth day of the march, he found it difficult to control his mind and began acting strangely. He was in a trance, later recalling only the motion of walking but was semi-alert to anything else. He kept moving, drifting in and out of consciousness. Charlie remembered coming out of the trance at a puddle of muddy water and he drank some. It revived his senses.

Later, he found it was not an uncommon occurrence on that march to have experienced a "walking coma," according to other survivors and medical experts.

Charlie's bedraggled column finally stopped at a railhead at San Fernando. Packed now into small freight cars they rode overcrowded for a short trip. Amid the intense tropical heat, no water was given for their trip to Capas. There last leg was a march to O'Donnell Prison Camp.

During the retelling of his Death March experiences—even after fifty-five years—Charlie said on some points, he just could not continue the interview, his memories were so horrible.

War reports of the Death March estimate that approximately 9,200 Americans and 42,800 Filipinos reached Camp O'Donnell, more than 16,950 having died from torture, murder, illness, malnutrition and hunger along the way.

As war crime records later bore out, General Homma ignored conditions for his prisoners and delegated the movement to his subordinates to carry out. After the war, the War Crimes Court held Homma fully accountable; he was executed.

Chapter 10 | In Captivity: Prison Camps on Luzon, Philippines

"In the early days of internment at Camp O'Donnell, Phillipines, men were dying nearly as fast as they could be buried. There was neither proper food nor medicine. An adequate supply of quinine and some meager food in those early days would have saved the lives of most, at least for the time being."
(War Crimes Report, Major Charles Underwood, Sept. 14, 1945)

O'Donnell Prison Camp
A.K.A "Camp O' Death"

Charlie arrived at O'Donnell Camp extremely dehydrated and barely able to stand, but alive! Japanese guards kept the men at attention in one hundred degree heat for over two hours. After a 100 kilometer march Charlie's feet were so blistered that just to stand now caused him excruciating pain.

O'Donnell Prison Camp was originally chosen by General Kawane of the 14th Japanese Army to hold an estimated 15,000 to 20,000 men, if improvements were made; it eventually held over 50,000 prisoners of war without any improvements.

The Japanese Camp Commander, Captain Tsuneyoshi, known for his anti-American sentiments, "welcomed" the men with a warning speech, labelling them as no better than dogs and saying they would be treated in such a manner.

The men underwent the ordeal of a second shakedown for personal articles. Any Japanese articles found resulted in severe beating or a firing squad, or both. If any POW needed a reminder of the harshness he was to undergo, the severed head of Captain Quiaiot had been hoisted on a front post for all to see as they entered the camp.

Through an interpreter, the camp rules were explained as the following:

—The Japanese Army does not recognize rank of prisoners of war.

—Prisoners will salute all Japanese officers and soldiers while wearing headgear and bow appropriately when not.

—Daily check-ups will be made for accountability of personnel.

—Men will not leave the barracks between the hours of 7:00 P.M. and 6:40 A.M.

—None will approach nearer than three meters to the fence surrounding the compound.

—Water will be economized. Only sponge baths are permitted, and very seldom.

—Anyone disobeying orders or trying to escape will be shot to death; most violations will result in firing squads or beatings.*

O'Donnell was a horrid place. The camp was on a barren field with a few bamboo huts and old barracks and tents, and surrounded by barbed-wire. There was only one spigot for drinking until summer. Soldiers waited hours to fill canteens. Waste removal was done by open trenches initially, and drew swarms of flies carrying germs that infested the mess halls and other areas. Not even livestock should be corralled in such a manner, thought Charlie.

—

*Office of the Provost Marshal General Report, Nov. 19, 1945, Am. POWs in PI

In Captivity

Charlie, and his buddies Tex, Gene, John, and Walt were assigned to a hut away from central activity and far from the normal path that guards checked. He slept on a straw mat. The hut leaked badly during the rain.

The morning formation saw a ragged group of stunned POWs. Charlie, like others, was in a state of shock, regretting surrender, thinking it would have been better to have died on the battlefield. They had no news from the outside world, no knowledge about their length of confinement. It was as if they had stepped into hell.

Three hundred POWs died of starvation and dysentery the first month. Charlie's daily portion was a handful of mucky rice, contaminated with worms and dirty. Dysentery, with its symptom diarrhea, affected every POW in the camp. Open trenches carried human waste, but waste was everywhere, as some men became too sick to make it to the latrines, resulting in acutely unsanitary living conditions.

After a month of the deficient diet, the men succumbed to other serious illnesses. Beriberi, an inflamed stomach and nerve condition, caused such stomach pain that a man could hardly walk.

In the first two months at O'Donnell meat was served only twice—in portions less than one inch square. Pellagra, which more severely affected the digestive system, occurred if the diet continued to be deficient. In addition, malaria was an epidemic problem.

1st Lieutenant Walt Scotty Strong, who marched with him on the Death March, died first. Walt suffered from dysentery, his symptoms progressed to Beriberi and he became weaker and was not able to stand. In a few days he could barely swallow. Charlie spoon-fed him camote (sweet potato) soup for two days. Walt tried to keep it down but couldn't. Charlie was holding him during a feeding when his last words came: "Charlie, I just can't eat this stuff." He turned his head and died. It was the afternoon of May 7, 1942. Wasting away from disease was far worse than being shot on the battlefield.

Each day Charlie detested his captors more, but there was little recourse for the situation; he learned to control his hatred. His goal was to remain in at least fair shape, and avoid becoming dispirited.

To visit with old friends and catch up on their news was the only promise of cheer. One friend was Johnny Olson. He had been at the battle of the Points. Captain Johnny Olson was acting as the adjutant under LTC Halstead, and had responsibility for compiling the morning camp attendance report.

In Captivity

Captain Tsuneyoshi, tyrannical about its accuracy, had no tolerance for an error in the headcount. Olson exercised the utmost caution in preparation; one error meant "suitable punishment" for him, in this case a severe beating or a firing squad.

Olson recorded the first days of activity at O'Donnell, in his remarkable book *O'Donnell, Andersonville of the Pacific* (1985). It begins with a description of Charlie's arrival.

——April 14, 1942: A group of approximately 1,500 brought into the camp around noon from Bataan. Officers placed in the area of the North East corner. Enlisted men placed in bamboo barracks east of service road. This was the first group from the Death March, and they arrived completely exhausted and suffering from malnutrition, as well as many from malaria and dysentery, but they were overall in much better shape than those to follow. Four men died.

——April 17, 1942: Due to the high amounts of sick, a "Bamboo Hospital" is organized by placing all medical personnel (medics) in bamboo barracks in north edge of the camp. Several more deaths occurred from malnutrition, heat stroke, malaria and dysentery. Medical supplies scant.

By the end of the month there were almost 8,500 POWs, and by the third or fourth month on, the population swelled with POWs from all over the Philippines and reached over 55,000.

At night, local Filipinos, sympathetic to the prisoners, tossed food, Spam, and medicine (including quinine) over the fence. Those POWs who walked near the fence did so at great risk; too close and a guard would shoot or cbeat him, but there were no other alternatives.

On May 7, 1942, men from Corregidor arrived. Although exhausted and in bad physical condition, they had at least been spared the cruelties of the Death March, putting them in a better position to withstand the rigors of the prison camp. The relative survival rates of the two groups bear this out both at O'Donnell and Cabanatuan.*

After the "starvation policy", further control was imposed by slapping, beating, torturing, and execution. If one violated a camp rule, the man was beaten and then usually went into "the hole", a small pit dug on the side of the slope, and was left there without food or water for days. To instill terror, the guards called out an entire section to witness the punishment. This was also used for an attempted escape, where the punishment was torture, followed by execution by shooting or beheading.

---

*Between 1942 and 1944, 2,399 men from Bataan died at Camp Cabanatuan and 237 from Corregidor (Office of the Provost Marshal General Report, Nov. 19, 1945, Am. POWs in P.I.)

In Captivity

Within O'Donnell a Black Market soon arose. If one had money or something of value to trade, a dose of quinine or food could be obtained. So Charlie, like the others, was forced to barter and scrounge. Charlie was a non-smoker, and on May 2, 1942, a Japanese holiday, the guards passed out a few cigarettes as a present from the Emperor—a perfect item for trading. That, and his other rewards, like a piece of fruit from the details he made, enabled him to obtain some food and medicine that kept him alive. Eventually Red Cross packages were permitted. In late June of 1942, the Japanese finally showed some concern due to the rising mortality rate and transferred American POW doctors who had been interned in Manila, and allowed medicine into O'Donnell. With professional medical attention and medicine, conditions and health improved, but their diet remained life-threatening.

Late in the summer of 1942, the Japanese closed O'Donnell as the major POW camp. Americans were transferred to another camp—Cabanatuan. After seven months at O'Donnell, Charlie was transferred to POW Camp Cabanatuan.

The black chapter on O'Donnell, a.k.a. "Camp O'Death", ended as the POWs left the main entrance of the camp. It had the dubious distinction of causing the deaths of over 1,600 Americans and 26,700 Filipino prisoners of war from starvation, disease and the brutality. Only a few medical and civilian units remained there to treat the men too ill and weak to be moved.

Cabanatuan Camp #1

Camp Cabanatuan was a large compound organized into three camps: Americans, Filipinos, and civilians. Charlie would be held here for the next fifteen months.

Most American POWs were assigned to Cabanatuan #1. They stayed in bamboo huts at one side of the camp, the other housed Japanese guards, and there was a section for the camp hospital.

The hospital was not in any sense a First Aid station; it was nicknamed the Zero Ward, because the gravely sick had about zero chance of living. The sickest prisoners went there to die. As at O'Donnell, the ward was filthy and corpsmen had to wait for rain water to wash the floors of human waste.

Cabanatuan compound was surrounded by a barbed-wire fence, guards manned the towers.

The daily diet consisted of a handful of mucky green rice a day, maybe one onion, and if lucky, a spoonful of meat—always animal guts. The burnt rice tasted like mud when warmed and served as coffee in the mornings.

As a result of the grossly inadequate diet, men suffered from all types of vitamin and mineral deficiencies. In the first month in

In Captivity

Cabanatuan, 503 men died of dysentery and malaria. Since the last days of Bataan, malaria was Charlie's worst tormentor; a mosquito borne disease, its parasite lies dormant for months, then erupts. Its recurring bouts—shaking chills, then high fever with flu-like symptoms and diarrhea—immediately required quinine, or respiratory and circulatory problems could lead to death. He relied on the local underground to smuggle medicine, and he needed food and money to barter for it. Filipinos working for the Japanese at Camp Cabanatuan smuggled food in for Charlie and others. Many POWs owe their survival to these brave locals.

Lieutenant Colonel Masao Mori, nicknamed "Blood" by the American POWs, was the Japanese camp commander. Colonel Mori's use of mass executions was the most unspeakable form of torture the POWs were to witness. For those that attempted to escape, punishment was beyond cruelty. If caught, one was first tortured, and then shot and those from the transgressor's section were severely punished—also shot by Mori's "shooting squads."

But the most depraved example Charlie witnessed occurred after a few months there. One day the POWs of Camp Cabanatuan #1 were called out and assembled in formation. Shortly the horrid scene unfolded. Two lieutenant colonels and a Navy commander had been caught trying to escape under a fence. They were beaten and dragged back, tied to poles and left in the sun and rain for two days—beaten regularly to the point where their physical features were unrecognizable, and then marched past their friends—one lieutenant colonel had an eye hanging down his cheek, another a broken jaw, the third a mangled leg. They were taken out to the woods and dug their own graves, Two were shot, one was beheaded. From then on "watches" from the American NCOs and officers patrolled the inside of the camp to prevent a fellow prisoner from making a reckless escape that put others in peril.

If the POWs were to survive at all, they knew they would have to improve the camp themselves. POWs with engineering, sanitation, and machinist backgrounds were recruited and dug irrigation trenches from the latrines, improving sanitation, and also rebuilt a defective pump which allowed water to flow from the water tower. Other POWs organized activities to keep their minds occupied, including a camp library, song club and horseshoe throwing club. Another group was assigned a task making street signs for the many lanes between bamboo huts, and named them after American states.

About the only kindness Charlie recalled was the International POW Notification Card. Since early 1942 his parents had not heard a word from him. They were elated when they received the next of kin notification card, with his signature (See Figure 12). Charlie also included a greeting to Gene Howe, founder of the Amarillo Globe News. Perhaps he wanted to remind Gene that he would need a job when the war ended.

In Captivity

Charlie had been a prisoner at Camp Cabanatuan for approximately sixteen months when he was told to get a "physical" for a transfer to Hitachi POW Camp inside Japan. Like most, Charlie welcomed the transfer to Japan, hoping for better conditions.

Figure 11: Camp O'Donnell (National Archives)

Deadline—Captain Charlie's Bataan Diary

Charlie Underwood Is Prisoner of Japanese

Capt. Charles C. Underwood, who was a member of The Amarillo Globe-News advertising department before he answered the call to colors, is alive, a prisoner of the Japanese.

For months, following the fall of Corregidor, the young officer had been listed by the War Department as "missing in action," but official news of his capture sent by the adjutant general's office to his parents, Mr. and Mrs. Ernest N. Underwood of Topeka, Kans., was relayed here this morning.

And so ends months of suspense, tinged only occasionally by doubt, for every member of The Globe-News family.

"'Little Charlie' is all right. He'll take care of himself."

That has been the oft-expressed fervent hope at The Globe-News office.

The army officer was known among fellow workers as "Little Charlie," to distinguish him from The Globe-News circulation manager, Charlie Underwood. The two Charlie Underwoods of The Globe-News are not related.

Capt. Underwood, a lean, lanky, effervescent and likable young man, who made friends easily had been associated with The Globe-News since his school days at the University of Missouri. He spent his vacations on the editorial staff. After he was graduated and commissioned a second lieutenant in the reserves, he was connected with the advertising department until Feb. 15, 1941, when he was called to active duty. He was stationed at Fort Sam Houston and when assigned to the Thirty-First Infantry he was transferred to Manila, April 21, 1941.

It was last Christmas that his parents received a radiogram announcing the officer's promotion to a first lieutenancy. He later was made a captain and the last direct word the Underwoods received was a letter, delivered last Feb. 15. The letter was written hurriedly from the field in Bataan.

"We've been in terrible suspense," Mrs. Underwood said to friends here. "Every contact I've tried to make through the Red Cross the letter came back. I finally did get a 25-word message on the Gripsholm this last trip. I hope he got it."

The news from Washington did not give the location of the prison camp where Capt. Underwood is held.

Two Amarillo young men, Brack Garrison and Gayle Neal, both marines, are in a Japanese prison camp from which radio programs are broadcast twice daily. Both of the Amarilloans have been "on the air" since their capture at Guam.

CAPT. CHARLES UNDERWOOD

Figure 11B: Front page headlines in *Amarillo Globe-News*

In Captivity

Below, Figure 12, is a copy of Charlie's next of kin notification card. It was sent in August 1943, to notify his family back in the States that he was still alive. Of note, Charlie sent greetings to Gene Howe, the founder of Amarillo Globe News. As indicated in the card.

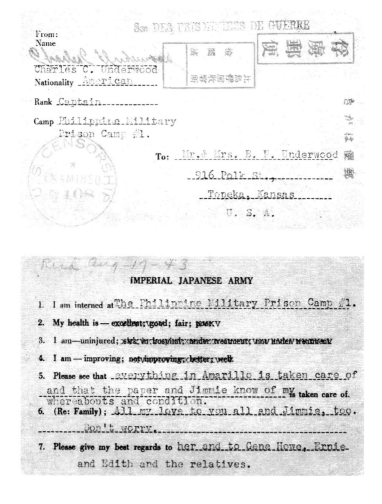

Figure 12: Notification Cards

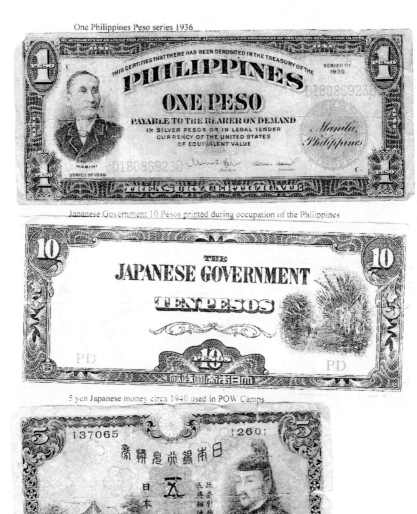

Figure 12B: Currency from Captain Charlie used in his third POW camp

Part IV

To Japan as POWs, Voyage on the *Taikoku Maru* and Hitachi POW Camp

Chapter 11 | The Voyage on the *Taikoku Maru*

In the first week of March 1944, American soldiers, considered healthy, were segregated for transfer to work camps in Japan and other regions under Japanese domination. Charlie was examined by Japanese doctors, who determined he was fit and capable of hard work. He was informed that he would transport to work in a mine as a forced laborer, north of Tokyo. Major Art Christensen, his former mentor, commanded the group. Officers were hand-picked. In March of 1944, three hundred men left Camp Cabanatuan for Manila. Never before had American soldiers been relocated as POWs to interior Japan. He was assigned to Camp Hitachi and remained there until the end of the war.

The POWs were herded like cattle into the non-ventilated cargo hold of a freighter, the *Taikoku Maru*, which set sail from Manila on March 24, 1944. Packed in like animals, it was not possible for all the men to lie down at once, so they slept in shifts. They sweltered from the tropical heat, were not provided drinking water, and became dehydrated.

The Voyage on the Taikoku Maru

On the second day out the ship encountered a typhoon, with winds over 55 knots and heavy cross seas. The rough sea broke over the deck and water gushed into the hold through a leaky hatch, keeping everyone cold, wet, and fearful of being shipwrecked. Sea sickness was rampant and most men caught colds, many even pneumonia. For human waste, a pot was provided in the hold, as the only latrine consisted of a shed built out on the deck, available for use only at certain times in daylight hours. The guards were also seasick and fearful for their lives and left the POWs alone to manage for themselves. The guards became relieved when the storm passed and began drinking. Inebriated, they threw bananas and fruit down to the POWs in a gesture of compassion. This was quite different from the experience on subsequent transport voyages where guards clubbed and shot prisoners or refused to render even water to drink. Uncomfortable as Charlie's voyage was, he later considered himself lucky. Other voyages with POWs fared worse. In December of 1944 he gleaned the first news, through a wireless story about, for example, the *Oryoku Maru.* It was strafed and bombed by American planes, wounding both American POWs and Japanese guards. After the air raid, U.S. medical personnel were ordered on deck to treat wounded Japanese, and then were beaten in retaliation for the attack by American planes. Aid was denied for the American wounded; they were left in the hold to fend for themselves. An estimated two hundred and seventy died. The bodies were dumped over the side into the sea by tens and twenties. (Japanese guards on the ship were later charged with capital war crime offenses.) Unfortunately, this was not an isolated incident: The *Shinyo Maru* sank in September 1944, and of seven hundred and fifty, only eighty-two survived. The worst maritime drowning of POWs occurred on October 22, 1944, when the *Arisan Maru*, transporting 1,782 U.S. and Allied POWs, was hit by an American torpedo. Only nine POWs survived. To hear of the death of his former CO, Captain Farrell, was a great loss. He died from suffocation on a transport ship.

Charlie's group disembarked in Osaka, Japan, on April 10, then went by streetcar to the railhead to board the train to Camp Hitachi. As they waited for the train's arrival, Japanese people observed the Americans with curiosity. Charlie believed they were the first Americans they'd ever seen. Major Christensen noted in his diary:

"As we waited civilians looked at us but were well behaved and did not bother us at all. We, on the other hand, were interested in seeing what the Japanese civilians were like—certainly, it appeared, not like the military! At one point the Japanese OIC gathered the Americans together and gave a speech. "Don't try to escape," he told us. "If you should do so, your leader (me) will be shot."

Chapter 12 | Prison Camp Hitachi

Figure 13: The POWs of Camp Hitachi: Captain Charlie Underwood is sitting in black pants, first row left with sunglasses.

The 302-man detail arrived at Camp Hitachi early in the afternoon of April 11, 1944. Known as Tokyo Camp D-12 (#8), it was located 70 miles northeast of Tokyo on the east coast of Honshu, on a mountain slope near the small settlement of Motoyama. The prisoners consisted of a combined force of American, Dutch, and English POWs (sixty-eight Americans, eighty-nine British and one

Prison Camp Hitachi

hundred and forty-five Dutch). Arriving at the camp, the men were tired, and many ill from enduring days of rain and the long cold travel to get there.

The conditions of Camp Hitachi were slightly improved over the other two internment camps. Here POWs were fed just enough to keep up their strength to work as forced laborers in the mine. The discipline was harsh, lack of food an ever-present problem.

Camp Hitachi was a stockade circle with barbed wire. The POWs lived in huts and referred to them as "cracker box houses." Water was readily available, as was electricity, most of the time. The civilian mine foreman, though Japanese, tried to be fair and humane. Some of the Japanese guards were fair too, though most were not. Twelve Japanese guards, including the camp commander, controlled the camp. There were three commanders during the internment at Hitachi: Captain Ryoichi Nemoto, Lieutenant Syokoi Matsuo, and Lieutenant Tjomahi Nakamura, who was in charge when the war ended. Guards either supervised in the mine or had duties at the camp. Some were retired Japanese soldiers called back up to serve as guards. Most of the "call-backs" seemed intent on proving their usefulness, and thus were brutal, by torturing defenseless prisoners.

Hitachi was small compared to O'Donnell or Cabanatuan. In a group of 302, it was much easier to be noticed, and selected out for "special attention." POW officers and men had the same guards every day. If a guard developed a dislike for a POW, he was then taunted viciously.

Upon arrival, Commander Nemoto ordered a welcome formation. POWs stood for hours on a cold raw day to hear his speech. Using an interpreter, Nemoto delivered the customary "welcome speech." It was derogatory and intended to both humiliate and terrorize the POWs, reinforcing their subordinate position. He called the men "lower than dogs," and concluded with a warning that the men would "never leave Japan!"

Next he reviewed the camp rules. He spelled out reprisals for infractions: Failure to salute a guard mandated punishment, attempted escape begat "suitable punishment"—death! In the interior land of Japan, of course, there was nowhere to go even if one did escape. Finally, POWs were only authorized to write notes about working in the mine.

Nemoto next described what was expected of the men. The POW's were there as forced laborers to mine copper for the Nippon Copper Company. Copper was used in a non-military capacity, such as for plumbing, "not for the war", he told the group. A quota of ore would be established by the mine engineer. Men were told that if they failed to work or interfered with work, food would be denied and harsh punishment rendered.

A Japanese named Queenie was introduced next as the camp

interpreter, Commander Nemoto said he was for the POWs benefit, to translate his orders so things ran smoothly. Queenie claimed to have had dual citizenship as a youth, and later told Charlie that his father was an American who had once worked at the American Embassy, and his mother Japanese. At the outbreak of the war, his mother decided to claim sole Japanese ancestry. Queenie's other brother had high status and worked for Domei, the Japanese propaganda and news bureau. Queenie got the latest news from both sides, and even an American Sunday newspaper, on occasion. The men knew, however, that Queenie was an informant who tried to play both sides, Charlie recalled later.

After the remarks by Camp Commander Nemoto, the Japanese guards took over and next came an hour of Japanese military courtesy. This lesson was taught by a portly guard named Kikuchi. Kikuchi, soon nicknamed "Heckler" by the men. He began the indoctrination on when to bow and salute. Prisoners had to salute all Japanese military and guards and bow for the Japanese camp NCO and commander. He then called up another guard to provide a demonstration. The POWs, who were already very tired, stood for over an hour practicing bowing while Kikuchi heckled each small group of men down the line as he observed the bows. Kikuchi had a glass eye and was blind from the left side. Thus, several POWs to his left were immediately accused of not bowing low enough and corrected by an open-handed slap to the back of the head by Guard Katzup Nagayama, or "Ketchup," as the men later referred to him behind his back. Ketchup was no joking matter but a beast of a bully, as they were to find out soon enough.

Next, Ketchup taught the art of saluting. A POW was required to salute every Japanese soldier or guard. Soon saluting became a form of harassment because of endless repetition. Another guard, Minrou Fugimoto, nicked named M.F. (and you can guess what that stood for), pulled a POW from the ranks to make a point. "This not how to salute," he said, "You are *bakero* (fool)." *Quack, quack* was the sound as he smacked the POW with a bamboo stick. Charlie, who remembered the bamboo treatment endured the day Bataan fell, found this distressing. "Here we go again," he thought. These three bullies worked as a team along with their leader, the assistant Japanese Camp Commander Tosho Mizumo (dubbed "Tiny Might" by the men he terrorized). Many were slapped before the formation was released.

The following day a civilian engineer from the Nippon Company was introduced to his new laborers. The first order of business was a very detailed indoctrination to the world of mining. The mine shafts were deep—about 160 meters down. Men scaled wood ladders to the bottom to dig for ore.

These lectures by the engineer and the mine foreman lasted about a week. The mine had marginal safety standards because of its age (over 50 years), and the mining equipment was obsolete.

The timbers that ran down the three shafts required constant reinforcement. Lighting was poor, headlamps were required but often failed, and there was no adequate air vent in the mine. In the summer months it was hot.

The engineer did not harass the men like the guards did. Working conditions were at times dangerous, especially when the temperature dropped below freezing at night causing the timbers to creak and shift.

The following is an extract from forced POW laborer Franz Adolf Lorzing, of the Dutch East Indies:

I did underground mining work 150-160 meters deep. The ventilation throughout the mine was so bad and it was so hot that you had to work completely naked, with only a Japanese cardboard helmet on and a pair of rubber shoes. The work that I did there was always hard with a lot of shifts. Among other things, it involved sealing old mine tunnels. The filling material consisted of mud and stones. The remaining space was so low that you scraped your back when, crawling like a snake, you had to push a flat truck, loaded with wet rubble, to the end of the tunnel where you had to shove the rubble in all the nooks and crannies. Then you had to crawl back with the empty truck. For years after the war, I had claustrophobic nightmares about it.

A couple of times I was in danger of losing my life. One day, fairly late in the afternoon, I was walking with three comrades through an old mine tunnel. Suddenly, the entire width of the tunnel collapsed in front of us. We ran back, but at the same moment a wall of grit and pieces of rock fell down and we were trapped inside a small space. Luckily for us, there was a waste chute connected to that part, we quickly removed this and crawled up the empty wooden chute. With superhuman effort, we managed to crawl to a tunnel higher up. Our mine lamps had gone out and in the pitch dark we groped our way along the walls toward the shaft openings where successive wooden ladders led us to a higher tunnel. After laboring for hours we finally reached the exit. In normal times we would have been greeted as heroes, but we were met with slaps from the Japanese guards because we were late.*

Camp Commander Nemoto, who had no mining expertise, organized the shifts by randomly selecting leaders. The Nippon engineer, however, did not see this as effective and preferred to select shift leaders himself, mainly from a group of American POWs who were stronger. The engineer politely implied that the Commander was meddling in his area. A heated discussion ensued.

---

*The extract above is from the memoires of the late Lorzing, courtesy of Michiel Busz as it appears in the Center for Research Allied POWs Tokyo #8B Hitachi, Motoyama formerly numbered 12-D, and is reprinted with permission by web monitor of pow1@mansell.com

Observing this discussion, American leaders caucused among themselves and came up with a creative proposal. It was diplomatically presented by Major Art Christenson to commander Nemoto—that the Americans would manage all work assignments in the mine, and would also fill the work rosters for all duties within the camp as well.

Key to this arrangement was Charlie's insistence that U.S. Officers be appointed as Officer of the Day, (OD). The OD was essentially a troubleshooter. His purpose was to solve issues which came up between the men, or problems occurring with the roster or problems with the men and their guards. While it placed an extra burden of the small group of seven officers it gave each a purpose. There were to be many issues and it kept the officers very busy. The POWs liked this proposal as it gave them a chain of command to which to voice their concerns. It was pointed out to all that the mine would run more smoothly and output of ore should be higher. The only thing Americans expected in turn was fair conditions and sufficient rations. But what finally sold the camp commander on the idea was when Major Christensen emphasized that as camp commander, Nemoto was *far too important a man to become involved in the small detail of selecting shifts.*

Nemoto liked the idea, and approved it. The Japanese guards did not. They saw the arrangement as usurping their authority. They constantly undermined the terms of the agreement. By retaliating against the POWs at any opportunity.

Morning roll call was at 0600 and began with attendance and an inspection, before marching out the gate to the mine. The first shift left at 06:30, the second at 07:30, the afternoon shift at 16:30 (4:30), and the night shift at 19:00 (7:00pm) The first week saw 260 POWs reporting for mine work.

Those POWs too ill for work, as determined by the Japanese doctor, would be excused from the mine and work on a camp detail. Later the American doctor was used but that met with contention from the guards. The morning guards inspected the men for necessary equipment and proper attire; any man lacking an item was slapped and told to quickly go get it. Each shift endured the same harassment. By the third week, the slaps had turned into beatings.

Privates Sedillo and Forrester (U.S.) came to formation with missing attire and were slapped. Later that day, Katzuo (Ketchup) found the men alone in the mine and hit them again, each in the face with his fist, three times. This occurred with others and always in isolation from other men. Complaints were made to Commander Nemoto, by the American senior officer Major Christensen. Nemoto pleaded ignorance to these incidents because he lacked any other witnesses to the act. Americans then requested a supervisor inside the mine, but were denied. The severe slapping continued and men used the "buddy sytem," as much as possible while in the mine.

Captain Charlie, recorded accounts of camp abuse. He kept his notes secret, at his own peril. He was very concise, writing only the date, time, event, victim, and guard. He used initials for the victim and guard. Later, delivered his accounts to the War Crimes Commission at the end of the war.

Figure 14: I.D. Photo's in Hitachi Camp. Capt. Charlie is the first man on the lower left #3774.

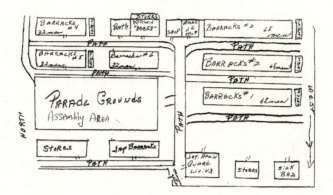

Diagram of Hitachi Camp 8, D-12 drawn by John M. Gibbs, as part of his Official report for the War Information Bureau submitted on July 31, 1946. The above designates the positions of buildings in the camp, all inside barbed wire. The floor of buildings was of sand and dirt. The sleeping areas in the buildings were raised about one foot above ground and an area of 30x72 inches was allowed each prisoner, storage space for clothing and mess gear was placed in the shelves above. The Latrines were at the south end outside the buildings. The smaller "barracks" contain 2 rooms and the larger one contained 5 rooms. The copper mine was located north outside of the barbed wire.

Figure 15 Hitachi POW Camp

Camp Duties

The huts were thin-walled shacks that required repairs and a heating source. 2nd Lieutenant Renka had craftsman's skills, and he made stoves from large tin cans. The American POWs worked better as laborers, because of their size, and did more of the heavy work. Whereas, the Dutch East Indies POWs, smaller in size, were found to be good at roofing the camp huts and stringing up electrical wiring. As the work was assigned, hard feelings emerged among the POWs. The task was to find a suitable duty for each to make a real contribution. Overall, each man worked to improve the camp's meager accommodation.

Electrical wires were strung to each hut, and evening lights—powered by a generator—were permitted for a couple of hours after dark. Trenches were dug to improve drainage. Important for sanitation was the number of latrines dug, usually at the southwest side of each hut. The latrines were not fitted with plumbing, and weekly the prisoners were required to shovel the excrement out to control bacteria and disease. They used sulfur for a disinfectant. Dr. Bahrenburg soon had his sick bay of sixteen beds up and running.

Adding to all these challenges was the management of the men. In the mine the shift comprised men of mixed ethnicities. Tired at the end of the day and poorly fed, the POWs didn't have the energy to do much in the evenings.

The largest threat to the health of the POWs in the early months was the chronic lack of food. Rations consisted of barley, rice, soybeans, sweet potatoes, some meat, fish and a few vegetables, estimated to be about 2,800 calories, or about half the rations necessary for performing a day's hard labor. Gene Conrad began to work in the kitchen—the food was horrible, and not much of it. The idea was to present a factual account of the acceptable calories needed (about 4,000) to perform hard labor, but Camp Commander Nemoto, but he was indifferent toward further accommodations requested by the Americans, much less food.

But the biggest obstacle to any significant improvement was the Japanese guards. They found ways to undermine any attempts at structure from the American officers. Commander Nemoto did not want to be bothered and delegated a wide range of authority to his assistant Corporal Tosho Mizumo. Corporal Mizumo took full advantage of the fact that he was second in command and he set a menacing tone in dealing with POWs. It seemed that guards competed in levels of cruelty to gain his approval. The worst of these were his four henchmen: Kogucki, Katzuo, Kozawa and Fugimoto.

The chief tormentors of men in the mine were Katzuo (Ketchup) and Minrou Fugimoto (M.F.). They liked to beat POWs for no or little reason. Ketchup in particular seemed to take delight in leaving a red bloodstain like ketchup on a POW's face.

These guards harassed men under the guise of "reeducation." They would prolong the formation before marching to the mine or at the end of the shift.

One day early in their stay, glass-eye Koguchi ended the day by forcing prisoners to stand in the cold for prolonged periods. Mine workers were dressed only in their lightweight summer uniforms that they had worn in the Philippines, and had no gloves. Then he ordered the men to stick their hands in the snow. This was called the "snow treatment." If one fell out during these educational formations, he was slapped, kicked or both.

Guards Ketchup and Kozawa often worked in tandem. Charlie was Officer of the Day one morning early in his stay at Hitachi when one of the worst tormentors, Guard Kozawa, under the direction of Ketchup, held up the men on a most bitterly cold snowy day. He forced the formation of sixty men to stick their bare hands, forearms, faces and necks in the snow for an hour. If you broke "formation," a beating occurred with a bamboo stick. Two Dutch soldiers fell and were beaten senseless and had to be taken to the sick bay for overnight recovery. This was the first example of mass punishment that occurred when the Camp Commander was not present.

The following week a group of eight men appeared for a shift without canteras (mine lamps), although lamps had not been issued to them. Ketchup called the men to attention and started beating two of them as an example: RAF C. Soon and Tam Choon. Noticing the delight of other passing Japanese guards, Ketchup then threw the next man to the ground, took off a shoe and beat him over the head. After forty-five minutes of this the mine foreman, hearing the cries, tried to intervene. He separated Ketchup from the POWs, who were finally permitted inside the hut to warm up from the cold. Shortly Ketchup returned and in effect said, "If you're cold, I'll warm you up." He forced them outside and slapped them for another twenty minutes. They were left standing at attention in the cold raw wind, while Ketchup went back inside the shack and built a roaring fire for himself. Then he went outside and had the men stand in the cold for about forty-five minutes in quarter knee-bends with arms outstretched before he released them. This was a second form of mass punishment. When CO Christensen complained to the Camp Commander, he was told dismissively that the "exercise" was a "lesson of reeducation in soldiering the Japanese military way."

On March 30 1944, a sergeant nicknamed Koots, a big hard-working American NCO, heard a wooden support crack in the mine and was directed to take his shift outside until the engineer could inspect the damage. Koots took his shift of twenty men outside in the direct sun to get warm, as it had been a very cold day. Ketchup came up and promptly gave Sergeant Koots a one-two slap on the back of his head with a bamboo stick. Koots saluted and inquired as to the reason for the slap. The men were moving around and some were jumping up and down trying to keep warm. Ketchup told him that was not a proper thing to do in formation. He next lined the men up facing each other in two rows and ordered them to slap each other about the shoulders and face. He said that was an old Japanese method of staying warm.

When the prisoners hesitated, he struck Koots again until the men reluctantly began slapping one another. The men were finally dismissed after thirty minutes, but Koots was held back and forced to work the second shift without food or water. He also sustained two more beatings from Ketchup, who said the man needed more training as a shift leader. That evening, Koots stumbled back to sick bay badly bruised and seeking medical attention; his face looked like raw hamburger meat. A strong protest was immediately raised by Charlie, who was Officer of the Day, to the assistant camp commander Mizumo.

The next morning at formation Mizumo (Tiny Might) addressed the shift of POWs and restated that the guards were there for re-education and did not like to punish the POWs and did so only when they committed an offense, then left.

The trouble was that "offenses" were imagined by their guards and the POWs never knew what they were beforehand, so prisoners were struck without cause. For instance, one day Heckler Koguchi, without explanation, slapped Dr. James Bahrenburg, Major, for "refusing an order." Later it was determined that Koguchi had never given Bahrenburg an order, but meant to.

Another time, in December 1944, Bahrenburg was passing the Japanese office and was accosted by Koguchi, who halted him and excitedly rambled in Japanese about saluting. From this, Dr. Bahrenburg deduced that he was supposed to have saluted as he passed the empty office, which had not been a camp rule. He then saluted Koguchi and was slapped three times in the face with an open hand. Dr. Bahrenburg never learned the reason for his punishment.

Brutality within the mine continued indiscriminately. On March 12, 1944, Minrou Fugimoto (M.F.) came to one of the shifts working in the mine and asked the Japanese sub-foreman if there were any poor workers. The sub-foreman said all work was good that day. M.F. persisted and asked who was the weakest; when Private Ralph Sedillo of the U.S. was pointed out, he sustained a vicious beating by M.F., using his fists and belt buckle. He was also kicked in the testicles and slapped repeatedly across his face with the blunt side of his bayonet. Ralph had to be assisted to the sick bay to recover.

There were guards that were more fair-minded, like Matsuda and Ishi. They were even kind at times to the men, and on work details outside the gate, Ishi would point to a plant or wild rice that could be used as food. But most guards were far from fair in their dealings with POWs.

It was very difficult for a POW to just stand by without redress and let another American or POW take a beating. Formal complaints were seldom investigated; nor did the beatings stop. The men just had to take it. If an American officer intervened, it was at his own peril and only to prevent serious injury or loss of life.

There were ways to outsmart the Japanese, Charlie thought. One hadn't endured Bataan, the Death March, and two earlier prison camps without becoming a little shrewd, and very tough. One day in April, the Camp Commander's short-wave radio was on the blink. Charlie volunteered to help and summoned an American radio technician called R.T. to fix the radio. He went with him, to supervise. He stood face to face with Nemoto. Suddenly, Captain Nemoto asked Charlie about fighting on Bataan. Charlie downplayed any combat role and said he was primarily an MP directing traffic in Bataan, and left it at that. At some point Charlie mentioned the need of warmer clothes and medicine, and found out wool clothing would soon be issued, but got no answer about the availability of medicine.

Radio fixed, Charlie and R.T. bowed and left. The radioman had made good use of the diversion and procured two supposedly "faulty" crystal tubes, which were later used by the Americans to make a tiny radio for themselves. At night when the coast was clear, they quietly turned on their tiny radio and heard updates about the war. Utmost caution was utilized, though.

The lack of food was always the problem. Underfed and forced to perform hard labor using a pickaxe and shovel required a proper diet for stamina—calories over 3000-4000 a day. The POWs received about half the necessary calorie intake to survive: soup in the morning and five spoonfuls of rice per man. At night it was fish powder or dried squid, or with luck a bit of fish. But all the food lacked essential vitamins.

The loss of weight had other health effects on the men. Many succumbed to diarrhea and beriberi and became very ill. The work roster shrank; more men went to sick bay. After many petitions, on June 1, 1944, Camp Commander Nemoto addressed the issue of the lack of food. He stated to the American officers that there was really no food shortage but that men were increasingly sick because of the Japanese climate change and because they did not properly chew their food. In early February squads of men passed out in formation because of malnutrition. Finally on February 12, 1945, less than one hundred ninety men were fit to stand work formation. Corporal Mizumo, acting as the camp NCO, stormed into the sick bay. He ordered the sick prisoners to stand at attention. Many were too weak and obviously unfit for work. A few could barely stand upright, yet he ordered all into formation for the mines. He then went up and slapped both Charlie, because he was Officer of the Day, and the American doctor, Dr. Bahrenburg, several times for putting the sick men on bed rest.

In mid-May Lieutenant Tex Evans was so ill with diarrhea, he could barely keep food down. This was Charlie's dear friend; they had together endured the darkest days of the Death March. He also remembered how his friend, Walt, died in his arms. He would not let this happen to Tex.

The American officers kept a small box of survival rations and he began pouring soup into the big Texan. Soon Tex was eating again. Flu struck the camp the following week. Then Earl became very sick and bedridden. Too many men were in a walking state of starvation.

A Change of leader for the POWs

The first major glitch to the "camp arrangement" came a few months after the Americans negotiated it. Major Art Christensen, the senior American officer, was transferred out along with Conrad and Evans to another camp in the north, Sendia #1 and #2, with a number of Camp POWs. That only left four officers to do the work of the seven officers originally assigned to Hitachi Camp: Captains Earl Short, Bill Nealson, (of the Medical Corps), Charlie, and 2nd Lieutenant Renka, who was just really learning about leadership. The doctor, Major Bahrenburg, was soon assigned to rotate between Hitachi and the Sendia Camps.

As a result a change of leadership occurred as Captain Earl Short, by seniority of time in his grade, was now the senior officer. Charlie and Earl were good buddies and neither broke stride over this, and like the others, just went to work as a team. Earl, at age thirty-two, was the oldest officer. This attribute grained him at least some measure of grudging respect among guards due to cultural respect for elders. Earl was fair-minded leader and a soldier's soldier, who had worked his way up through the ranks, having been at one time an admin clerk for MacArthur. He would enjoy a remarkable Army career over of over thirty years. Charlie had known him in the 31st Infantry before the war as a close friend and they'd bumped into one another in Manila when Earl was looking for crates to bury the 31st Infantry ceremonial punch bowl. They were also at Camp O'Donnell and Cabanatuan together. When the Japanese Camp Commander finally permitted an America officer to go and observe activities in the mine (May 1944), Earl went first himself, then rotated between Charlie and Nealson. That did not, however, deter problems with the guards.

It was also about this time that Commander Nemoto was transferred back to Tokyo. He was replaced by Lieutenant Matsuo. Commander Matsuo relied heavily on his assistant Corporal Mizumo and there were no improvements in the treatment of the POWs. In fact, he elevated Mizumo (Tiny Might) to the assistant commander and allowed him to make more frequent use of corporal punishment. As expected, the new Commander began his tour with a shakedown inspection of certain camp areas. In the officer's hut, clothes were thrown about in a search but nothing was found. The morning formation was kept waiting for over an hour.

Charlie was no longer a young innocent junior officer. Having survived Bataan and the Death March, he had matured beyond his years to a hardened combat leader. The men from Bataan were a separate breed and knew it. Those men were devoted to Charlie and respected his boldness. Charlie was not cocky but had for the most part figured out how much he could push his Japanese oppressors. He knew one had to show strength, to gain their respect.

All American officers tried hard to be impartial in their dealing with the mixed ethnic group that formed the POWs of Hitachi, and seemed to be well-liked by the respective ethnicities. To one another the officers became like brothers for life; each watched out for the others.

News and Rumors

In a prison camp men are desperate for news—any news of outside events. Most of the time news takes the form of rumors. As mentioned, Queenie was an unreliable source. One Monday after the morning formation, Queenie came to Charlie and announced that things would get better. Emperor Hirohito had ousted War Minister Tojo, he gleaned. The information proved true, though it was not confirmed until much later; but it was the first instance where Queenie began to share accurate information with the POWs. Charlie saw this as a turning point—reliable news would be forthcoming, and with it came hope.

There were other ways to obtain information. A British Malaysian POW by the name of Ry Singh was chosen as the unofficial U.S. interpreter. He could speak and read Japanese and became invaluable. For instance, the Japanese guards were sent lunches, wrapped in newspapers, from the nearby village of Motoyama. After lunch, the newspapers were trash and discarded. At night the papers were collected and pasted together by the Americans. Singh translated them, and passed on the latest news. Since he wasn't American, the early question was, could he be trusted?

Deciding to use caution, at first American officers censored their conversations around him, perhaps unjustly. His newspaper translations proved accurate, however, as determined by the hidden radio. Then Singh was used as a check on the reliability of Queenie. As the war got closer to mainland Japan, Queenie became more vocal reporting on the latest Japanese losses and bombings, heard from his uncle who worked for the propaganda office Domei in Toyko.

Routines and work proceeded smoothly in early spring of 1944, but given the temperament of camp guards, Charlie knew it would not last long. Soon he himself became the center of a dispute.

It began May 28 1944, when one of the worst beatings of prisoners occurred, involving Private Jean Guiraud of the U.S.A, a mine worker. Guiraud was a very good worker. A Japanese-Korean mine guard one day started to harass him and raised a club to strike. Guiraud, trying to protect himself from an undeserved beating, put his hand up in defense. This was seen as defiant. Also, the Korean accused Guiraud of striking him—which was not true. Ketchup and Kozawa were called in and Private Guiraud was subsequently beaten unconscious in the mine. He was then awakened with a douse of cold water, dragged from the mine, and beaten and kicked until he admitted he'd tried to strike the mine supervisor.

Guiraud was covered with blood and lost consciousness a second time. They doused him with water and revived him. Guiraud was next brought to camp and made to stand at attention in front of the Japanese guardhouse from 3 p.m. to 6 p.m. During this interval, all members of the Japanese guard—ten in number—repeatedly took turns striking him with fists, rifle butts, boots and boards, and beat him a third time into unconsciousness. They then threw buckets of cold water, but it did not revive him. Charlie arrived on the scene as they began to kick him. To prevent a death by beating, Charlie had to do something, so he stood in front of Guiraud and waved his hands, shouting, "No more, no more." The guard immediately ran to the Camp Commander. Charlie expected to be slapped for intervening—but that went with the territory, he thought.

However the camp commander summoned the three officers, wanting to set an example. Within minutes the three stood before the camp commander and were introduced to the "roundhouse ordeal." First, the officers were berated and cursed—its intensity heard throughout camp. The captains were accused of undermining the guards' authority. The gang of five guards circled around like sharks and proceeded to knock the American officers around, beating each with fists, bamboo sticks, and boots until each dropped. Nealson got a tooth knocked out, all sustained bruised hamburger-like red faces, swollen jaws, and sore ribs.

Charlie felt very bad that his two colleagues were caught in the crossfire, caused by his own decision to intervene. Private Guiraud survived his vicious assault. He, and others, believed the intervention had probably saved his life, and the story spread over camp. Shortly afterward, a man came up and sketched Captain Charlie. It was the only drawing of an American officer made by POW Ferdi.

The three officers had been well-liked by the men, but from that day on were admired even more, because every man knew they had their support.

Figure 16: Drawing of Captain Charlie Underwood, as a POW in Hitachi Camp, by fellow Dutch prisoner Ferdi, January 1945.

If an injured person required treatment in the sick bay, and many did, Charlie went down and offered compassion, and also ensured the injured POW would not go haywire and try to escape. Not only did that provide aid and comfort, it permitted Charlie to gather first-hand evidence to later submit to the War Crimes Commission. The POWs knew he was a writer, and he had made a promise to them to bring charges against the abusers. Somehow the men felt a little better after his visits. Those POWs, who were frail and weak, like many of the Dutch East Indies men, did not fare well. Of the one hundred fifty Dutch, most were in pitiful shape and could not withstand a beating—five died the first year.

Food Deprivation

In Captain Charlie Underwood's War Crimes report on the subject of food he wrote: "The shortage of food at Hitachi was a continuing and severe problem. The diet was no better than at Cabanatuan Camp and the effect perhaps worse because now men were forced to perform hard work laboring in the mines. Thus, the situation was always grave, starvation ever-present, then disease common. Men were too ill to work, but were forced to work."
The shortage of food began early after arrival into the camp, as noted by Charlie:

April 14th 1944, all POWs went down the hill in the rain to begin lectures on mining operations. Many men suffered from colds and diarrhea due to poor diet. Fed watery soup for lunch, small sweet potato—most inadequate diet.

April 20th 1944, first day in the mine for the men—a sixteen hour day. Officers set the shifts, assign men to shifts, but stay in camp. Men are exhausted by the end of shift, given a teaspoon of salt afterwards. Fed gruel in the morning and watery soya paste soup for second meal.

April 29th 1944, Emperor's Birthday. As a special celebration, no work and was allowed to purchase in "camp store" two badly bruised oranges and two cigarettes, smokes useful to barter...

May 6th 1944, nothing much to eat this past week, but barley and a cupful of soya bean paste, per day. We are all very hungry. Brain became light-headed when making up the roster, or with any work. At night dreamt of food. Weight dropped. There has not been fish or meat for over three weeks. Men suffering from diarrhea, drinking water is suspected among other things.

May 11th 1944, received Red Cross package—what a delight: powdered milk, powdered (instant) coffee, small can of SPAM—first taste of meat in almost a month.

With the inadequate diet, Charlie's health, like the others, began declining. He awoke one morning with blurred vision. It didn't go away, and by noon he just could not see. He was escorted to sickbay—he had incurred vision-blindness similar to nyctalopia from a condition caused by a chronic vitamin deficiency, which can be fatal. Charlie was helpless as a baby for over a week, and had no sight for several days. His morale sank but he was reassured by the American doctor—if they could only get him some real food, he'd be okay. Charlie was dependent on the good nature of friends. They immediately came to his aid. Earl Short, for example, cheered him up by reading aloud to him—*Horatio Hornblower*, and *Men Against the Sea* (a sequel to *Mutiny on the Bounty*), Charlie remembered. Next they found a bit of fish, and then killed a rodent. It made up only a few bites but it helped during those pitiful days. Dr. Bahrenburg, arriving from Shinagawa Hospital, Tokyo, brought with him a supply of much-needed vitamins. That, and the "better" diet ended the symptoms of nyctalopia after a week or so, and Charlie resumed his duties.

On 17 October 1944, the camp received the first meat in over a month—70 kilos of fresh salmon, 15 kilos of beef, and 40 kilos of "old beef and pork entrails." The new camp commander, Lieutenant Matsuo, took half of all provisions for his 12 men and left the other half for 295 prisoners.

Captain Earl Short kept a hidden diary and wrote in it when he could. This would prove important as both an historical and an evidentiary source. His annotations described the events of the day, recording the problems, the abuses, and the deaths. Captain

Charlie kept notes of the mistreatment of the POWs; each officer hid his notes from the Japanese. Here is an excerpt from Short's diary, as carried later in the *San Antonio Evening News*, November 8, 1945:

6 July '44. Men have not had any meat or fish now for six days. Our issue of vegetables was nothing more than a large white radish. Imagine eating nothing else but radishes and maize for five or six days.

Japanese Medicine: Lectures, Torture with Burning Cotton Balls.

It was the policy of the Assistant Commander Mizumo (Tiny Might), to "discourage" a man from obtaining medical treatment and to force the sick POW back to work. The Nippon Copper Company had their own doctor but he made irregular visits. Men deemed "unfit for duty" were few. Those who were found to have a pretty serious injury were reassigned temporarily to the sick bay. Others were put on kitchen detail, or sent out to care for the animals. And they were always subjected to harassment by roving guards. The camp commander insisted, regardless of how widespread illnesses were, that no more than ten percent of the men could ever be declared "too ill to work."

When a man was too ill to make morning formation, he first received a "motivational lecture" from one of the guards. If he failed to return to work after that he was then slapped, by hand or in some instances a bamboo stick.

On July 4, 1944, Sergeant Thomas E. Buchanan (U.S.A.) sought treatment of a severely sprained ankle. Tiny Might found him lying in bed. He questioned Buchanan, who said he could barely stand on the foot. With that, Tiny Might maliciously twisted the injured ankle several times, and said in effect, "I'll show you what a painful foot is."

On July 9, 1944, Sergeant Estil J.Coheen (U.S.A.) broke his toe in a mine accident, and went to sick bay. Tiny Might confronted him the next day, ordering him to get up. When he hobbled, Tiny Might stepped right upon the foot with his boot, inflicting severe pain. He said "You a baby, you need to know what real pain is!" When the Japanese camp doctor cautioned the guard, he too was threatened as an "interferer," and he backed off and denied Coheen needed medical attention.

On December 15, 1944, De Greet and Doornweerd, Dutch POWs, reported to sick bay with pneumonia. Corporal Mizumo slapped them until they rose and staggered back to work. The U.S. Officer of the Day made a valiant attempt to reason with the Corporal Mizumo, but was slapped several times himself for interference.

Denied medical attention for a life threatening illness, both men collapsed within hours in the mine. De Greet died later that evening on the 15th and Doornweerd on the 16th.

There were Japanese remedies to motivate the POWs who sought treatment. Most horrific were the flaming cotton balls, an unorthodox treatment dispensed by Mizumo himself, who had no medical expertise.

On February 7, 1945, again, Tiny Might ordered four men suffering from the intestinal disorder (beriberi) to forcibly undergo the hot cotton burning. U.S. Warrant Officer H. Wilkinson, Dutch Sergeant Will De Gruiter, Dutch Private Pieter Von Winger and Dutch Corporal Von Galen were held down by two guards while golf ball-size cotton balls saturated in alcohol, were placed on their bodies and set afire. The smell of burning flesh and their outcries were gut-wrenching to all nearby. Captain Nealson, the duty officer of the day, staunchly protested this action. Corporal Mizumo would not stop, and continued "the treatment". A protest to his superior, Lieutenant Matsuo, also fell on deaf ears. Lieutenant Matsuo told Nealson something to this effect: "This is an old Japanese remedy, I approve of it." The men, of course, showed no improvement after the burning and bore scars. It was only toward the end of captivity that very ill or injured POWs received acceptable medical care and only when referred to the hospital near Tokyo.

The worst case of lack of medical treatment occurred with a Dutch soldier named Edwards. On February 28, 1944, he awoke with severe pains in his side. Corporal Mizumo denied treatment and forced him to work in the mine for two days until he collapsed. He was carried out to sickbay and remained unconscious. He was then removed to a Japanese hospital near Tokyo, where he died the next day on March 1, 1945. He was found to have gangrene throughout his abdomen due to a ruptured appendix. Only a small box was returned with his cremated remains. This was one small box that Charlie never forgot about. Brees, another Dutchman, died March 15th of pneumonia. Below, Figure 17, is a photo of Hitachi Camp Sick Bay. The quality is poor, it was likely taken with a homemade camera after the Japanese surrender.

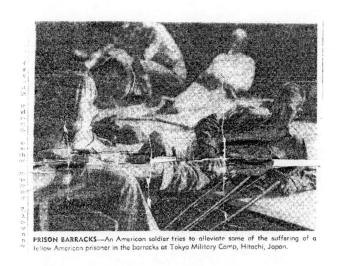

PRISON BARRACKS—An American soldier tries to alleviate some of the suffering of a fellow American prisoner in the barracks at Tokyo Military Camp, Hitachi, Japan.

Figure 17: Hitachi Camp

Chapter 13 | Charlie as Camp Mess Officer

"Luxurious Dining. We are having grasshoppers today. We have eaten some strange things since the war began, including snake, lizard, monkey, horse, mule, caraboas, cat, dog, civet cat, silk worms, guts, blood, fish heads and now grasshopper...It can't get worse." *
—Captain Earl Short (*San Antonio Evening News,* Nov. 8, 1945)

Upon his recovery from temporary blindness, Charlie wanted to improve nutrition and food in the camp. He volunteered to be the mess officer in charge of the kitchen. He would be in charge of food preparation and supplies.

Prior to this, Charlie knew little about cooking and nothing about running a kitchen. He took taught himself everything from A to Z about food preparation, because lives depended upon it.

Charlie as Camp Mess Officer

As mess officer, his shift began early in the morning and ran until the evening. Charlie had to select his cooks and kitchen details. He also dealt directly with many Japanese in and outside the camp—drawing rations from Nippon officials on a bi-monthly basis. He was also in charge of accountability of these items. Charlie quickly discovered the facility was in a real mess.*

When the Americans' arrived, Japanese Sergeant Dono had oversight of the kitchen; he regularly stole food and supplies, and then lied about it. Then he used his authority as a supervisor to elicit a witness from the other guards to falsely blame a POW for taking the missing item, and was thus despised as both thief and tattletale. His actions were responsible for a number of POWs getting slapped. The first week of Charlie's new job, Dono accused him of stealing two cups of powdered milk and a few potatoes. As this was a serious offense, the commander investigated and found Charlie's whereabouts were accounted for, and Charlie heard no more. Shortly thereafter, Sergeant Dono was "promoted" out of the kitchen to another assignment.

---

*See Appendix II: Prison food summary prepared for the War Crimes Commission by Captain Underwood

Saburo Kozawa, cited earlier for his brutality of many POWs, became Charlie's new supervisor for the kitchen and storehouse. Kozawa expected unauthorized meals, which stole food from the men's share. He'd come to the kitchen for a bogus "inspection" in the afternoons, expecting food. Using tact, Charlie prepared only a light snack of soup and very watery tea, then stopped the practice altogether by July, by scheduling kitchen maintenance during the late afternoon break period.

The word soon got out that Charlie refused all demands for unauthorized food, even by the guards. Within days, however, guards began taking out their displeasure on his kitchen staff. Koguchi, the Heckler, came in the kitchen in January 1945 and accused the American Sergeant Coombs of disrespect, when he failed to render a salute. Coombs was working the grinding mill and had not heard the guard enter. This explanation failed to satisfy Koguchi who slapped him about fifteen times. He said "although Coombs was a big man he could handle him."

Charlie's policy was to stay as businesslike as possible with all and avoid all familiarities. Though he got into numerous arguments, on only one occasion was he manhandled in the kitchen. One day the assistant commander, Tosho Mizumo (Tiny Might), entered the kitchen and started an argument over whether to add garlic to the noon meal or the dinner meal. He did not like Charlie's answer and used that reason to hit him repeatedly with his wooden clipboard in front of his men. Like a bully, Tiny Might did such

Charlie as Camp Mess Officer

things only when the commander was out of the camp on other business.

When Charlie first took over the kitchen, he had a crew of nine men of mixed nationalities. Five were good cooks in pretty good physical condition. The other four were sick men sent from the mine whom he took in, in their weakened state. Gradually, seeing the benefit of this, the Japanese replaced his cooks with more sick men who could not work in the mines. Some of these were uninterested in kitchen duty. While Charlie accepted some of them, he was also very firm and refused any freeloader. Finally, the Japanese allowed Charlie to pick six men of different nationalities, as long as he selected no men in key mine jobs.

The Mess building consisted of two parts: the larger dining hall where men ate (and also took shelter during air raid drills), and the kitchen, which had an old stove, no refrigerator, and a sink and cupboard.

On September 10, 1944, someone broke into the storehouse and stole sugar and potatoes. The American officers were ordered to conduct a search among the POWs and found nothing but part of a broken lock near the Japanese guardhouse, indicating that the guards themselves were the likely culprits. However, the camp commander would have none of it. Prisoners were denied noon and evening meals and Red Cross cigarettes.

The next day the commander told Charlie he would be held responsible for total accountability. Charlie worked to stop the pilferage and felt his personal safety depended on stopping it. A week later, a small group of Dutch POWs were found to have stolen ten sweet potatoes; they were held in a prolonged formation and beaten by the Japanese guards. The camp commander told Charlie that if this ever happened again, he would be severely beaten. That night Charlie went around and talked with the Dutch POWs. He explained the situation but added they too would be severely beaten if pilferage failed to cease. They liked Charlie and readily agreed and were true to their word. This was the only known food pilferage that occurred while Charlie was in charge of the dining facility.

Some resentment existed against the Dutch prisoners, especially those from Java. They had their own set of values and initially lifted an occasional article that was not in use. Only once did a serious altercation take place between an American Sergeant and a Dutch junior lieutenant protecting his men. Charlie had to break up a near fight over a borrowed headlamp. After a discussion and warning from Charlie, whom they seem to respect, peace was restored and the Dutch POWs were able to control this urge. This appears to be the only exception to discipline within POW ranks in nearly eighteen months in Hitachi. It was the Japanese guards as well at the Nippon mine suppliers who were the real thieves.

Charlie dealt directly with the mine company's food supplier and requested more vegetables, meat and fish, with varying results. He and Earl worked in unison and submitted recommendations to the camp commander. Most fell on deaf ears. It seemed they could never convince the Japanese that they would achieve better results in the mine if they would feed the POWs properly. Nonetheless, Charlie achieved improvements, and one had far-reaching benefits for the POWs.

One major improvement Charlie instituted was the charting of food statistics (also see Appendix II). To put anything in writing violated camp rules. So approval was obtained from the camp commander to allow food and calories to be written in clear sight on a board. For example, in November 1944, every man got a daily ration of 2,845 calories, 10 percent of it protein. During the month, meat was served three times at 200 grams a portion, fresh fish three times at 222 grams and dried fish three times for 89 grams. Then that was correlated to "sick days" of non-work for POWs to demonstrate that healthier men had fewer sick days.

Secondly, Charlie uncovered the fact that the way food was measured caused a shortfall. The Nippon mining provisions were delivered in kilos based on head count. The total amount given was shared with the Japanese soldiers, who received a higher portion. The sick POWs got even less, as is pointed out already. Fraud occurred with each delivery. Often goods were skimmed off the top before delivery.

Soon, Charlie discovered that the mining company used a "light kilo," which they called the "Irish kilo," in their measuring. Charlie found this amusing, since the Irish were not on the metric system at all in the 1940s; the bogus measurement had likely been invented by the mining company as a good way to shortchange everyone. Charlie promptly pointed this out with a demonstration.

The next delivery, Charlie boldly informed the Nippon supplier that as mess officer, he would under no circumstance accept the "Irish kilo," and demanded delivery of a full kilo, or advised him to take it up with the camp commander. Charlie was adamant, but trembled when he stood his ground. He pointed to the weight scale as he measured out the evidence. All hell broke loose from the Nippon supplier! The commander stormed down to the kitchen with heat in his voice; he demanded an explanation for Charlie's "interference." The consequences would be severe for him, if it did not work in his favor!

Charlie very politely gave a demonstration, measuring out flour in standard kilos in one pot and the shorted version of the Irish kilo in another. The camp commander was a man who did not like to be shown up by any American—but there before him was the evidence: They were the victims of Nippon Copper Company fraud. The commander turned to the mining supplier, growled out a line of profanity, and dismissed the man after a stiff warning. The Nippon supplier returned with a gift of another bag of flour. The commander approved. Then, looking back at Charlie before he left,

Charlie as Camp Mess Officer

he gave him a warning: Holding an imaginary pistol close to his head, he pulled the trigger. Charlie knew what he meant. Close call, Charlie thought. That week, he had won a small victory, but he knew he was a marked man from that day on. Guard Kozawa watched him like a hawk does his prey for about a week.

Another improvement was a change in the Japanese Camp system of dispensing only half-rations to the ill prisoners in the sick bay who were too weak to work. This made no sense at all, as pointed out by Dr. Bahrenburg, Charlie and Earl. They finally convinced the camp commander to give out three-quarter rations a day for an ill prisoner.

With these improvements, for the first time, prisoners, as well as their Japanese captors, had almost enough food, and enjoyed the quality. As the meals improved and men's weight held steady or actually rose, their morale improved.

One morning in early February of 1945, Charlie probably pushed it a little too far. A Colonel Sucoma from the Tokyo Military District came to inspect the camp. Before Hitachi he'd been to the nearby camp of Chinese POWs. It was filthy, their food was maggot-infested and the sanitation was in a deplorable condition; they'd had over 150 deaths due to disease. When Colonel Sucoma arrived at Hitachi Camp, he went right to the kitchen. He first studied the dietary charts, looking them over one by one. The colonel seemed to be impressed that they listed daily calories and correlated this with the health of the men. He saw this as an educated approach to running camp mess.

He spoke very good English and asked about camp food. Charlie answered, truthfully, "The men are still hungry, and need more food. With more food the mine output would be higher, sir." The Japanese colonel was somewhat startled by his assertiveness but reflected on Charlie's answer. The colonel stated that he agreed and would check into this and come back on his next visit.

The next week, on February 13, Commander Matsuo reassigned Charlie out of the kitchen. Matsuo expressed his "appreciation for Charlie's service," and explained his policy was to change officers in their administrative duties about every six months. It had been seven months. Later, Earl and Charlie chuckled over the fact that the commander had told Earl he'd reassigned him because "Charlie argues too much, won't keep quiet, and doesn't do what he is told."

Second Lieutenant Renka assumed mess duties until Charlie was eventually reinstated out of necessity. Renka attempted to take up where Charlie left off, but did not have the officer experience to control the forceful guards. Soon pilferage resumed on a wide scale and the food quality dropped; they were back at square one—on a starvation diet. Red Cross packages with canned food were a staple now, but far too many packages were confiscated by the guards for themselves, who also began starving.

Second Lieutenant Renka was reassigned to constructing needed heating stoves, and he performed very well, making six barrel-type stoves.

Chapter 14 | Christmas Season 1944 and Red Cross Packages

At the start of the Christmas season the first two deaths occurred at Hitachi Camp. De Greet and Doornweed, both from the Dutch Army, had died from conditions of forced labor on December 15th and 16th, respectively. They were cremated and their ashes collected in a small jar that was kept in the officers' hut as a sad reminder until buried outside the camp a few days later. See photo below of the camp burial formation (Figure 18)

Due to the deaths, morale was very low around Christmas; more deaths were anticipated if conditions did not improve. The cadre of five American officers worked as a team to improve food, conditions in the mine, and treatment from their captors. Charlie, like the others, tried to put on a positive mood for the sake of the men in camp. The officers felt a celebration would improve everyone's mood. The Japanese commander agreed to a holiday on Christmas.

A call went out for auditions for the Hitachi Christmas Choir.

Christmas Season 1944 and Red Cross Packages

Captain Bill Nealson, who had band and choir experience, was delegated to handle this festive event. The Japanese commander seemed amused as Earl Short explained the nature of the intended celebration, which was a non-Japanese custom, but approved the Christmas celebration show.

Within a few days of the announcement, over twenty volunteers assembled for the one permitted rehearsal. The musical choir included the popular Dutch, British and American Christmas carols. The Dutchmen sang soprano, whereas Americans and British were comfortable with alto and bass. The results made for

Figure 18: Burial services for POWs Ede De Greet and Theo Doorweed, December 18th 1944. Printed with permission, Center for research Allied POWs under the Japanese

a melodious performance; most of the men were moved by it. After the concert, Red Cross boxes were given to the men. Later, American prisoners and the officers were escorted in small groups to the Japanese orderly room. On an old Royal typewriter they were allowed to type a two-line "greeting message" on an International Red Cross card that was to be sent home. Had it not been for the recent Dutch deaths, it might have been an enjoyable experience.

The Japanese camp commander pulled Captain Nealson out of a morning formation a few weeks later. He gave him ten musical instruments with orders to put on a show the following day for Japanese VIPs to celebrate their national holiday. Captain Nealson had not held an instrument in over three years. Nonetheless, he knew it was useless to protest, so the following day he and nine other men conducted an even better musical arrangement than the caroling at Christmastime. It was great for morale.

Red Cross Packages

The International Red Cross (R.C.) parcels were delivered to the POWs, as approved by the Japanese War Ministry. The packages contained essential foodstuffs such as powdered milk, crackers, cheese, canned ham, candy, cigarettes and the like, and maybe a paperback novel. Some Red Cross parcels even contained clothing.

Christmas Season 1944 and Red Cross Packages

The senior POW officer signed for receipt of the packages, and that slip was then returned to the Red Cross as evidence of proper delivery. A total of six deliveries of parcels were received from May 1944 to August 1945, most arriving in the spring and summer of 1945. Red Cross packages were sent with advance notification. When word of its arrival came, it was like receiving a Christmas gift—such joy!

The Japanese camp commander made the announcement a few days before the date of delivery. Hitachi guards teased the prisoners at that point and said that the "packages were intended for only the better workers who did not go on sick call."

A day before the packages were officially received, guards usually passed around American cigarettes (from the new parcels) to men who in their opinion were considered "good workers".

The following day the R.C. parcels were distributed. More often than not, men received pilfered boxes and it was a big disappointment. When the men complained, their protest fell on the deaf ears of the camp commander. In other instances, the camp commander gave the American senior officer little choice in the matter, by saying, "Sign for these or they will go to another camp." The guards hoarded the packets themselves and on one occasion the camp commander himself was found leaving the camp carrying an armload of new Red Cross parcels.

Chapter 15 | Spring 1945
Contact from the U.S. Air Corps

"On June 14, 1945, one bomb hit the mine. The damage closed down a shaft. The men had gone through a lot by then and it would be a pity, I thought, if they got killed by our own Air Corps."
—Interview with Colonel (ret) Charlie Underwood, 2004 with the author.

For the past year, black-out drills had occurred in the evenings. Men would drop everything and form up inside the Mess Hall, all crowded together in complete darkness. In late spring of 1945, American B-29s began regular bombing runs on Tokyo and northern industrial targets.

On the June 14, an American B-29 found the range and dropped a lone bomb on the mine, causing a secondary shaft to cave in. The debris was cleared in a day or two, and mining continued. A week later, a U.S. fighter plane swooped down on the camp and the men hit the ground. They'd been sprayed with bullets several times before but this time the plane flew low and they saw the American

Spring 1945

decal on the plane, a P-47 fighter, and were relieved. Later, a work detail left camp to scrounge for wild rice and edible roots when another B-29 flew over taking a low-level observation. The next day another B-29 dropped several canisters with parachutes. They gave instructions to paint in large white letters "PW" on the roofs of the buildings to avoid an aerial bombing, anticipated in the near future. The camp's location had now been confirmed as holding POWs.

Due to the frequency of these fly-overs, Japanese Commander Lieutenant Tjomahi Nakamura, newly assigned as camp commander, expressed no objections to painting "PW" on the roofs. His acquiescence signaled to the Americans that the tide was turning for the Allies.

Other changes occurred. Medical care which had been denied was suddenly available. POWs who sustained injuries were taken directly to the hospital in Tokyo for treatment. Twenty-eight POWs went to the hospital on the first day! Upon return they spoke highly of the care received as well as sharing the latest news. The city of Tokyo had suffered widespread damage by American bombers. No doubt, the U.S. Army was coming.

But the path to liberation had unintended consequences. Food supplies delivered by the Nippon Company became irregular. Even the camp commander had no notice when a food truck was to come.

From mid-July on, the air drops of food became more essential and frequent. Canisters contained chocolate, Spam, crackers, cigarettes, clothing and an occasional magazine. Luther Bass, an American POW, made a flag from parachutes carrying one such canister. In 1973, Earl Short donated the flag to the Truman Library.

The Japanese guards knew a change was imminent; all they had to do was look skyward to see the American planes flying over their territory, but they outwardly dismissed its effect for weeks, until the morning that the camp commander ordered Charlie's kitchen dietary charts to be burned. Fortunately, most of the paperwork was preserved. Keeping his own counsel, Charlie had kept most of those records hidden at a secure location.

On July 17th, 1945, the mine was bombed a second time and sustained severe damage. It was at this time that the Nippon Company feared that their trucks would be bombed on roads, and ceased supplying food to the camp. With no means of resupply, the men went on half-rations. The camp was now virtually dependent on aerial food drops from U.S. planes.

Ministry of War: Japanese Kill Order for All Allied POWs

At the end of July 1945, the concealed radio held by the Americans in camp reported that the Japanese Office of War Ministry had

Spring 1945

issued a decree: the order directed camp commanders to kill all POWs if Japan was invaded by the U.S. Army. In August that order was amended to kill all POWs as a final disposition regardless of whether an invasion occurred.

That followed a U.S. Army forces report of a mass execution back in December 1944 of Americans at Palawan Camp, Philippines. There, an estimated 141 men were slaughtered in a trench. First sprayed with gas and ignited, prisoners who tried to escape the flames were shot down by machine gun fire.

Given these events, the situation at Camp Hitachi became very tense.

Chapter 16 | The Surrender of the Japanese at #8 Camp Hitachi

The morning of August 10, 1945, was unusually quiet. The 0630 hour daily formation had been delayed. Camp guards were absent.

At 0730, a POW reported seeing Guard Ishi very upset as he ran into the camp commander's office. A rumor spread quickly that all POWs would be assembled for the purpose of mass execution.

Unknown to the POWs in Hitachi, at the same time at Camp Zentsuji American officers had been assembled and stood at attention. Facing them, a cadre of Japanese marched out armed with rifles; bayonets were fixed and pointed at their throats, prepared for the "final" order which did not occur.

At 1030, the Japanese camp commander "asked" to meet the U.S. officers. Shortly, and with great trepidation for their personal safety, officers assembled in formation to meet the camp commander.

The Surrender of the Japanese

Lieutenant Nakamura, in full dress uniform, including his military sword, walked out. The commander was visibly tired. He marched up to Captain Short, bowed, and said that the Emperor had agreed to an armistice with the U.S. Forces. He had been ordered to surrender to the nearest available American unit. He handed over his sword to Earl Short.

Captain Short, in total surprise, showed his professional nature and immediately took the sword and stated that he would assume command of all Japanese forces at Hitachi.

Captain Short asked, "If the Americans leave this camp today, will we be safe among the Japanese people?"

"No," Lieutenant Nakamura replied. "I cannot guarantee your safety. Recent bombing by U.S. planes has made the Japanese people angry at Americans."

"Is there any communication with American forces?"

"No," answered the Japanese officer. "All messages are now discontinued with even higher Japanese command."

He stated that many Japanese soldiers were fleeing to the countryside. The Japanese War Minister had encouraged guards of POW camps to flee. He thought Hitachi guards would stay, as Emperor had rescinded that order and directed all Japanese to fully cooperate with the Americans. "We expect fair treatment,"

Nakamura said with temerity as he left.

In a matter of minutes the tables had completely turned—well, almost. American officers were equally astonished. Control of the camp did not immediately transition to the American officers. The Americans had waited over four years to be free, whereas the Japanese were in disbelief after hearing of the surrender, but obediently followed the orders of their former camp commander.

Many POWs urged taking the Japanese guards into custody, some calling for them to undergo a firing squad. There was one problem with that. The guards had kept their weapons! This made the truce an unusual one. So Americans kept watch over the Japanese allowing them movement in camp. Neither side knew exactly what to do or how to treat the other side.

American soldiers painted larger POW signs on roofs everywhere and waited for a friendly plane to fly over and drop more food. They fixed the radio so they could receive messages. The Americans knew U.S. forces controlled most of southern Japan, but there was no direct means of communication. The men anticipated being liberated by U.S. forces in a day or two and waited anxiously. Yet the radio still transmitted hostile Japanese directives issued by the Japanese Minister of War.

Thus began a strange détente that lasted nearly a month. Both POWs and Japanese guards. Utilizing the established military

The Surrender of the Japanese

structure, the Americans took control of the camp. Now the Japanese acted friendly. For instance, the bully Fujimoto approached former prisoners and apologized for his slapping and beatings, stating that he would never do it again. Camp Commander Nakamura politely requested individual conferences with each American officer. When they met he apologized to Charlie for his "stay" at Hitachi. Nakamura claimed he had only been following orders from the war minister. Charlie, cool to his approach, acknowledged only his part in the smooth surrender of the camp, but also reminded him of his command duties, denial of food, and the many beatings that he should have stopped. After that, Nakamura held no further meetings.

During this transitional period, Charlie took charge as mess officer again, and began to improve the quality of the men's diet. He and Renka had the kitchen running smoothly, but there was too little food until, after a search, the Americans uncovered hidden stockpiles of grain as well as vegetables, sugar and beans.

Weather permitting, U.S. fighters flew over the camp daily and and dropped small bundles of canned chocolate, coffee and newspapers. There were also large food drops from Army B-29s about once a week.

While the Americans of Hitachi Camp waited for an expected rescue, Charlie documented evidence against the guards.

Deadline—Captain Charlie's Bataan Diary

Figure 19: Newspaper article about food drops at Hitachi Camp

The Surrender of the Japanese

By August 17, 1945, Charlie had a staggering amount of evidence against seven Japanese guards. The most egregious charges involved the deaths of the five Dutch POWs. Mizuno, the Assistant Camp Commander, had denied medical care and treatment to these sick POWs and, in the men's eyes, he was believed responsible for those deaths. He was kept under close supervision. But each Japanese guard was concerned that charges would be brought again them, and as such avoided the company of other guards for fear of guilt by association.

By August 27, 1945, the men of Camp Hitachi still waited for rescue by American forces. The Japanese acted friendly now. Most U.S. men gained weight, particularly after two weeks of regular meals, yet some were still very ill. and were "hospitalized" in the sick bay. Some American POWs wanted revenge on their former Japanese guards, or any Japanese soldier—a very common reaction upon release, but this impulse had to be squelched.

After more than three weeks with no communication from the American landing force, doubts of rescue surfaced. Was it only a ceasefire and not a full surrender? News of the Japanese unconditional surrender finally came over the radio on September 2, 1945. The men wondered what was happening. Food supplies were dwindling.

"Charlie, we got a situation. We've got to notify someone we're here and get help," Captain Earl Short told Charlie at the end of the first week in September 1945. There was only enough food for a few days and as many as fifty men badly needed medical care. Charlie and Earl surmised that the American Army advance had stopped at the port city of Yokohoma, south of Tokyo—an overnight train ride from Hitachi railhead.

Charlie volunteered to take the train. He would ride it back until he found the forward line of the American advance. By "take," Charlie meant "commandeer the train." Earl would ready the men for their march to the railhead.

Chapter 17 | Commandeering the Train

"Still no word from U.S. Army about our release. Captain Charles Underwood with one Marine (Bernie), one soldier (Koots), and one RAF interpreter (Singh), and one Japanese guard left for Tokyo or further to contact American lines to acquaint them with our plight, obtain provisions and make arrangements."
—Captain Short's diary, 6 September 1945

Before Charlie left for the train his friend, Captain Short, warned him: "Stick only to that mission, don't worry about anything else, and for God's sake, don't fail to return."

With a small detail, Charlie went to Mutuyama, the nearest railhead, to convince the Japanese trainmaster to allow them to commandeer a train to U.S. lines. He handpicked the tallest American soldier to appear intimidating: Army NCO Koots and the Sergeant Bernie Christie, a Marine NCO; the interpreter, Singh; and finally one Japanese guard, Ketchup. Ketchup's presence made the detail appear as an official American-Japanese group,

Commandeering the Train

meeting in Japan. Charlie instructed Ketchup to be on his best behavior as a representative of the Japanese army.

At the railhead, the trainmaster required convincing. The bespectacled Japanese engineer said it was nearly impossible to travel to Yokohama, the American front lines. He warned that the plan was crazy, "Only Japanese—here, here, and here, all the way to Yokohoma." He warned them of marauding Japanese soldiers and malcontents. Only a "special train has permission to go Yokohoma!" he advised.

Charlie was determined. Singh translated that his detail would take control of the the caboose and telegraph ahead. Charlie told the trainmaster to telegraph all points along the route that the caboose held the highest military ministry and was not to be interfered with. The train rolled out of the station with the Jpanese and U.S. guards posted at the doors of the Caboose.

The trip was tense. After an hour, the train stopped in the middle of nowhere. It chugged on for another thirty minutes or so. Go, then stop, they proceeded by fits and starts. At every pause the detail tensed in anticipation. As they passed through towns they saw crumbling buildings and bombed out neighborhoods caused by U.S. aerial bombing.

At the first roadblock a uniformed soldier armed with a rifle stood on a rock mound. The train was forced to slow to a snail's pace.

Charlie's detail stood just outside the car door at attention, revealing their rifles; the rail-guard saluted as it went by.

At another point along the track, Charlie heard the sound of gunfire in the distance. He noticed straggling Japanese soldiers wandering like vagabonds, removing their uniforms to blend in with the civilians.

At a stop in Mito, passengers attempted to climb on board the cabooseuntil they saw the guards. A uniformed rail-guard checked the train, looking inside the cars as he walked toward the caboose. Charlie prepared for a possible confrontation. Instead, Singh greeted the train guard with the rehearsed story that they were important military ministers, U.S. and Japanese, heading to a meeting with General MacArthur. The guard nodded and walked away.

Finally, during nightfall, they approached an urban area where there was a checkpoint manned by U.S. soldiers—the outermost limit of American forces. The train slowed. An American sergeant was surprised to see U.S. forces on a train from the north. Confused by Charlie's appearance, with his outdated insignia from the Philippines, he didn't salute.

"Are y'all GIs?" he hollered in a thick southern accent. NCO Koots responded, "Holy Christ, we damn sure are!" and that bit of old-fashioned American profanity snapped the checkpoint soldier into a belated salute. The American soldier looked initially bewildered, but then yelled: "All areas south have been cleared," he said, then gestured ahead, "the depot area is another twenty kilometers down the track."

Shortly the train pulled into a military loading area where soldiers in U.S. Army-green uniforms were at work. A greeting came from a Lieutenant Thompson, the officer of the day, the first American officer they'd seen in almost four years.

Charlie immediately briefed him on the urgency of the mission and requested provisions and medicine for the men left behind in the POW camps. Thompson shook his head and said that special approval was required to procure provisions and that was beyond his authority. Charlie sternly advised him to "call his damn boss on the horn, because he planned to load the train with needed supplies with or without his approval."

The lieutenant ran back to a control office; after an hour, he returned with a very improved attitude. Apparently, he had doubted Charlie's story, given his ragged uniform and gaunt appearance. From the list on his clipboard, he read off Charlie's name—still listed as captured. "Amazing, Major," he addressed Charlie, then explained that an Army list confirmed Charlie now as a major, a promotion. Charlie had not heard about this, of course.

Loading the train car with supplies would take about twenty-four to forty-eight hours, the lieutenant said. He offered to get Charlie a new uniform and a good meal, and handed him paperwork to fill out to request the load. Charlie had no time for paperwork. He threw it down and said, "Lieutenant Thompson, if General Douglas MacArthur were here himself, how long would it take to form a detail and load this train with provisions?"

"ASAP," Thompson shouted at attention.

"Right," Charlie continued with a raised voice. "Now, I am on the direct staff of General Douglas MacArthur [which was not exactly true]. If you value your career or have any hope of returning to the United States on your normal rotation, you will help. Right now you are obstructing my need to obtain medical aid and food for starving American POWs interned for nearly two years."

"Yes, sir, I understand, but there are other issues. With all due respect, sir, we are awaiting a Status of Forces Agreement with the Japanese. The train schedules are technically coordinated with the Japanese trainmaster."

The Japanese trainmaster was immediately summoned. Speaking Japanese, Charlie snapped him to attention. He looked like one of their camp guards. Charlie informed him that he was on the staff of General MacArthur. Instantly, the man began quivering and bowing every few seconds. At Charlie's direction, Singh informed the man how pleased General MacArthur would be to discover a prominent Japanese train official fully cooperating with this small request.

The rail car was loaded with rations, uniforms and medical provisions in two hours. During the loading, Thompson arranged for Charlie's men to be fed and made comfortable. When asked, Charlie had only one additional request: one cold beer each for himself and his POW soldiers. An MP captain arrived prior to their departure with maps and photos. He gave a short intelligence briefing on where pockets of Japanese resistance had been reported, pointing out where Japanese soldiers were still adhering to the Bushido Code of never surrendering and still fighting. He advised caution in these areas.

With a final requisition of a few defensive weapons, they prepared for departure. The trainmaster designated the train an express and said there should be no problems on the nonstop run back to Hitachi. Charlie hoped this would be the case.

The train moved swiftly out of the depot. Charlie's four-man detail had performed well. He did not realize that Thompson would give a full report to the General Officer, Command level, which was then picked up by the *Stars and Stripes* newspaper's far east office.

As the train started back to Hitachi, Charlie exhaled a sigh of relief and felt a sense of accomplishment, but he was not home yet. He posted his soldiers at the front and rear of the train and ensured that the detail was still at a high state of readiness. Their one Japanese guard, Ketchup, was growing uneasy; Charlie advised his men to supervise him closely.

The first few hours of the return trip passed without incident. Near Mito, the train entered the mountain region. Crossing the bridge over the Kuji River, Charlie heard a loud commotion and thought a supply crate had fallen, he was startled by a scream. Singh jumped to investigate; in seconds, he was back. Out of breath, he exclaimed, "The damn Jap Ketchup fell or jumped from the train!"

Rushing forward, Charlie peered down into the ravine. Far below was the lifeless resemblance of the body of Ketchup. The train never stopped.

Koots had been the only one close by. "What the hell happened?" Charlie demanded. Koots, explained that Ketchup apparently fell when the train lurched. He hadn't actually seen it and could make no official statement about it. Had the guard followed the Bushido Code to never surrender? Charlie could find nothing more to clear up this incident.

The rest of the trip passed without incident. Upon return to the Motoyama railhead the men at Hitachi were fed, and the following day boarded the train back to Yokohoma. To their amazement, a grand welcome reception greeted them in Yokohama. They were met by General Eichelberger, the U.S. Area Commander, a full military band, and Army nurses.

Charlie had done his job. One of the first groups of American POWs was liberated from north of Tokyo. The men were bused to the base military hospital shortly after arrival.

There were other POW camps north of Hitachi, and Charlie again volunteered to take the train and liberate his comrades at Sendai Camps 1 and 2. The train was provisioned and a second detail volunteered, commanded by Charlie. The second journey was easier than the first trip; it lasted two days and encountered no problems. The Sendai POWs were elated by their arrival.

Back in Yokohama, the military brass decided that the men would not be released; due to their gaunt appearance, they looked too ill to be seen by the American public. Most prisoners had lost at least a quarter of their normal weight. Charlie was down to 110 pounds from 155 pounds. The ex-POWs were directed to recuperate for thirty days and fatten up. The men immediately protested this command restriction. After what the men had been through, the men wanted, and were entitled to, their freedom. That restriction was dropped after a week. What probably helped was the call Captain Earl Short received from General MacArthur, who also thought the former POWs should have their liberty.

Charlie postponed his celebration and immediately went to the base's staff judge advocate officer, who handled military legal affairs. The military attorneys read Charlie's documents. By the time Charlie left a few days later, charges against seven former Japanese guards had been approved for War Crime Court proceedings.

Within days the men boarded a Navy transport ship, the *USS Dyckman*, and sailed back to Manila, before proceeding to Hawaii. The accused war criminals of Hitachi Camp were taken into confinement at Sugamo Prison in Toyko.

While back in the Philippines, Captain Short had an "urgent mission" on Corregidor Island: to reunite the 31st Infantry with its cherished ceremonial punchbowl. When General King announced surrender of the Bataan Defense Force on April 9, 1942, it was Short who had buried the Shanghai Bowl and cup set so it would not fall into Japanese hands. The bowl figured prominently in the much-decorated regiment's ceremonies. In mid-September of 1945, by permission of the commanding general, Captain Short returned to Corregidor Island with a small detail; he dug, but was unable to find the bowl. The excavation was continued by others until it was located in December, 1945—just a yard and a half from where Captain Short remembered it to be. Below is a copy of the

Commandeering the Train

correspondence regarding the retrieval of the 31st Infantry's Shanghai Bowl below.

FROM: GENERAL HEADQUARTERS
UNITED STATES ARMED FORCES, PACIFIC
A.P.O. 500
16 September 1945

TO: LT. GENERAL W. D. STYLER
COMMANDING GENERAL
UNITED STATES ARMY FORCES, WESTERN PACIFIC
A.P.O. 707

Captain E.R. Short, who has just been recovered from a prisoner camp in Japan, buried the 31st Infantry Shanghai Bowl on Corregidor shortly before the fall of Corregidor- I am sending Captain Short to Corregidor to locate the place where he buried the Bowl. Request that you furnish him with transportation by fast boat to go over on the morning of 17 September.
Also request that the commanding officer on Corregidor be instructed to furnish labor, tools, etc., to assist Captain Short in excavating the Bowl.

/s/ R.J. MARSHALL
Major General, U.S. Army
Deputy Chief of Staff
FROM: GENERAL HEADQUARTERS
UNITED STATES ARMED FORCES, PACIFIC
MILITARY INTELLIGENCE SECTION, GENERAL STAFF A.P.O. 500
28 December 1945

Deadline—Captain Charlie's Bataan Diary

TO: MAJOR EARL R. SHORT
910 Colita Street
San Antonio, Texas

Dear Major Short:

The undersigned was a member of the party which accompanied you to Corregidor in September, last, when you pointed out the location where you had buried the 31st Infantry punchbowl and cups.

The area marked by you was excavated and the trophy was not found. The engineer Lieutenant who had been present when you pointed out the approximate location of the punchbowl telephoned about further investigation. I made another trip to Corregidor and pointed out where it appeared that further work might lead to success. Again nothing was found.

It still seemed to me that digging should be continued. I suggested where it should be done. It will interest you to know that the punchbowl and 65 cups were found about a yard and one half to the north of the area selected by you for excavation. The punchbowl was recovered in good shape, as were all cups.

With the season's greetings, I am,

Sincerely yours,
/s/F.T. Armstrong
Colonel, G S C Exec. O., G-2

In Honolulu, Charlie and the other men were lodged in the luxurious Royal Hawaiian Beach Hotel for a week awaiting stateside passage. Finally, the men boarded passage on a merchant ship to San Francisco. Observing the condition of the men, the ship's captain allowed his galley to stay open twenty-four hours a day, much to their delight.

In San Francisco, physicians met them at the dock, intending to confine them to a recovery ward at Letterman Military Hospital. The officers protested and left the hospital with or without medical consent and went into San Francisco and had a hell of a celebratory party. Every bar served free drinks.

Chapter 18 | The War Crime Charges

There were hundreds of Japanese soldiers charged by the War Crimes Commission. Among them were General Masaharu Homma of the 14th Imperial Army, who had overall responsibility for the forced march of prisoners called the Death March, as well as Lieutenant Colonel Masao Mori, commander of Camp Cabanatuan, and Captain Tsuneyoshi, commander of Camp O'Donnell. All three were found guilty and executed. General Homma underwent the ordeal of a firing squad; the others were hanged.

According to the U.S. National Archives, in the War Crimes Trials at Yokohama, 327 cases were brought before the tribunal, and a total of 1,037 Japanese were prosecuted between 1946 and 1949. Six of the Japanese guards from Hitachi Camp were charged, and were incarcerated in Sugamo Prison, Tokyo.

Sugamo, built in the 1920s, held political prisoners of Japan in the 1930s and 1940s. It was not damaged during the USAF bombing of Tokyo. It remained under American military control from 1945 to May of 1952, when it was returned to the Japanese at the end of the occupation and eventually torn down.

Charges and verdicts against the Guards of Hitachi Camp #8B

Under the War Crimes Commission Act, alleged atrocities were Class B, defined as conventional crimes against humanity, and Class C crimes which include the planning, ordering, authorizing, or failure to prevent such transgressions. The three camp commanders were charged: Captain Ryoichi Nemoto, First Lieutenant Syoko Matsuo, and First Lieutenant Nakamura. Prior to Court, and without consultation with any American Officers (POWs) of Hitachi, Nakamura was released. The reason given was his short tenure as commander, the lack of severity of his offenses, and his cooperation toward the Americans when Hitachi surrendered. Other guards charged were corporal Toghio Mizumo, Saburo Kozawa, Minrou Fujimoto, and Masatumo Kikuchi.

Copies of the original charges against two of the Camp Hitachi guards are reproduced in Appendix I.

Case Number 166, 1946 was assigned as the trials of guards of Tokyo #8B Hitachi. In layman's terms, the commanders were charged for their policy of torture, and failure to discharge their command duties to provide humane treatment to prisoners in that they carried out systematic starvation, ill treatment, denial of medical treatment, and compelled American and Allied POWs to perform as slave laborers in the Hitachi Copper Mine, in violation of articles of the 1907 Hague and 1929 Geneva Conventions for the treatment of Prisoners of War.

Each offender had the benefit of a military and Japanese attorney. Most pled not guilty to the allegation of violating laws and customs of war, each claiming they were following orders. The two officers stood stoically, and had little to say.

When Kozawa was tried on twenty-three specific charges he trembled. His charges were the willful torture and mistreatment of twenty POWs by striking repeatedly with bamboo clubs, beating ten into unconsciousness,; striking another twelve with the butt of a rifle; striking four American officers in the face with fist, bamboo stick, and boot; igniting gas-soaked cotton balls then applying them to eight POWs; stealing and depriving fifty POWs of Red Cross food parcels; kicking fifteen POWs in the groin; and other forms of cruel acts such as the "snow treatment."

The War Crimes Charges

Upon hearing these charges, Saburo Kazawa, the notorious bully of Hitachi pleaded for mercy. Next was Koguchi, who claimed his innocence because he had a glass eye and said he couldn't tell the effect of his beatings.

Copies of the original charges against two of the guards, written by Charlie, are included in Appendix A.

The verdicts were as follows:

Captain Ryoichi Nemoto: Guilty of six of sixteen charges, sentenced to hard labor for three years.

Saburo Kozawa: Guilty of thirteen of twenty-three charges, sentenced to hard labor for twenty-three years.

First Lieutenant Syokoi Matsuo: Guilty of nineteen of thirty-seven charges, sentenced to hard labor for seventeen years.

Corporal Toshio Mizumo: Guilty of seven of nine charges, sentenced to hard labor for seventeen years.

Minrou Fujimoto: Guilty of seven of twelve charges, sentenced to hard labor for fifteen years.

Masatumo Kikuchi: Guilty of six of seven charges, sentenced to hard labor for twelve years.

After sentencing, prisoners were sent back to Sugamo prison where they were to serve out their sentences. By 1950, however, the Japanese reaction to the Tokyo War Crimes Tribunal was increasingly negative and demands for pardons grew. In 1950, a Japanese political movement demanded the release of B and C class war criminals. Asserting the unfairness of the War Crimes Tribunals based on relaxation of standards regarding primary evidence in the proceedings, and citing the "misery and hardship of the families of war criminals, due to the harsh sentencing." The amnesty movement quickly garnered the support of more than ten million Japanese.

On March 7, 1950, MacArthur issued a directive that reduced the sentences by one-third for good behavior and authorized parole after fifteen years for those who had received life sentences. Most Japanese war crime prisoners were released at that point, and cases that had not yet been tried were dropped.

On September 4, 1952, President Harry Truman's Executive Order 10393 established a Clemency and Parole Board for War Criminals. It recommended following recommendations by the Government of Japan for clemency, reduction of sentences, or parole for Japanese war criminals.

Chapter 19 | The Transition

The transition from POW to active army soldier was a difficult one. Most of the Hitachi POW American officers, including Charlie, stayed in military service and made a career of the army. They had been like brothers for the past three years, and would maintain frequent contact with one another for the rest of their lives. In fact, they met informally on a yearly basis. These informal meetings helped them process the war traumas. These contacts served as a way to check in, to see that everyone was okay, just as they'd done in prison camp. It was a way to "cover their backs," a habit so ingrained from their years of incarceration that they would never forget it.

After the war, Charlie was selected for Advanced Officer Training, then earned his master's degree in journalism from the University of Missouri. During one spring break he visited Gene Howe at the Amarillo Globe Newspaper, and chatted with friends and reporters there. In that short visit he realized he was now more suited for a military career.

His next assignment found him commander of a regiment in Germany. After command time, he was subsequently selected for many senior military courses and key assignments, including a rewarding tour as the military attaché for Turkey in the early 1960s.

After that, to his surprise, he was selected to assist the Japanese—now our close ally—in planning for a Pacific defense. One night, at a diplomatic party hosted by the Japanese in Washington, D.C., he sat at a long dinner table across from a pleasant-looking Japanese diplomat. "Colonel," the Japanese official asked, "have you ever had the pleasure of visiting my beautiful country?"

Slowly, and in a steady dry voice that was unique to Charlie, he answered. He briefly mentioned his wartime experiences, including his time as a guest at Camp Hitachi. The diplomat became profoundly quiet, then came to attention in his chair and bowed to him. "Colonel, it is most regrettable that I ask you. Please forgive me, sir," he said.

"The Japanese people are proud of their new country," was Charlie's sole reply.

Perhaps hardest of all was forgiving the Japanese military. But after World War II, a great change occurred in the Far East region, and General MacArthur's policies facilitated rebuilding a new democratic Japan.

Charlie's next assignment was as the Information Officer at Ft. Sam Houston, Texas. In the early 1970s Charlie worked directly for the Commander in Chief Pacific, Admiral J. McCain, Sr. (Senator John McCain's father) at Camp Smith in Hawaii, before finishing his career as the Information Officer at Ft. Shafter. There he resumed writing and reporting stories involving military affairs, completing a "full circle" of a career, so to speak.

Like others in his small group of friends from WWII, Charlie's post-war achievements put him miles past the horrid experiences of Bataan and prison camp, turning those nightmares into distant memories. He retired in San Antonio, Texas.

For the small group of ex-POWs, what was amazing was how well they transitioned and dealt with their war issues. There were probably two reasons: first, these friends bonded for life, and, second, each one of this small group of young men had major accomplishments in their futures. Years after the war, Charlie, Earl Short, Gene Conrad, Matt Dobrinic, Johnny Olson, and Art Christensen continued to move up the ranks in the Army—all had impressive military careers, achieved the rank of full colonel and were esteemed by their peers.

The Transition

After military service ended, Charlie and the rest of the former officers of Hitachi continued their tradition of informal annual meetings. It was such a joy to see one another. Central to their visits was always a discussion of keeping America strong and limiting the exposure of young soldiers to war on foreign soil.

Figure 20: Colonel Charlie, age 43, and Mrs. Underwood, in happier times. February, 1963.

Chapter 20 | Interviews

In 2004, Charlie Underwood, now a retired colonel, gave his first war interview with the author. Charlie talked nonstop for three hours, discussing the campaign on Luzon and Bataan in detail. He gave another taped interview in 2005 with Brian Carr, PhD. Below are a few of his comments that shed light on Charlie's views during his war years.

What did you think of General Douglas MacArthur?

I thought very highly of him. America has never had a general of his authority. He was both a statesman and a commander. The Filipinos idolized him and saw him as their supreme leader; the Japanese feared him. He assumed U.S. command of the Philippines probably too late and inherited a mess. He was absolutely shocked at the poor state of our equipment. He opted for an offensive war versus a defensive war when his predecessor advised the opposite, and in theory that is the only way to win a war. As the hostilities began, we were all caught off-guard and had pre-WWI equipment. As the war turned in our favor in 1944, MacArthur's island-hopping strategy saved time and saved lives, probably mine included, as at that time POWs were starving in POW camps.

Did you have any dealings with General Wainwright, or other Generals?

General Wainwright was a hands-on general, a staunch and beloved field-fighter, visible to the men as much as possible. I was impressed with Wainwright and attended some of his staff briefings. I knew his aide Tom Dooley, and his G-2 Joe Chabot, both fine officers, and was well-informed about our tactical situation as I traversed Luzon. General Jones, my commander, was a take-charge guy, more like a Patton, a great tactical leader I also admired. He was a colonel, commander of the 31st Infantry prior to the outbreak of the war, and rose to two-star rank by January of 1942. He knew his men and he knew tactics. His advice should have been followed more. These generals were excellent field commanders and led from right up on the front lines. They'd be in the foxholes with us. When we went on half rations, they went on half rations.

In your opinion, what was the situation at the time of surrender?

The decision to surrender was about the darkest day of my life. We followed the order of our commander—but surrendered thousands of troops. Troops were very ill and demoralized and starving. You don't win wars by surrendering. Had we any indication of what was to follow, in hindsight, it was a mistake. The March was horrific, and to the man, none of us wants to think back on those dire days. But I would never surrender again.

What do you most recall about the Death March?

I don't want to recall anything. To recall anything about the March is still difficult. I will only mention a couple things more.

The road was very dusty and we were so very thirsty. The need for water was great. On the second or third day of the march, we passed by a warehouse where much of our food still sat in storage. It had never got down to the men. We starved on Bataan. We that survived the March relied on the buddy system.

Interviews

What do you recall foremost about your experiences in captivity in the prison camps?

Our captors were attempting to just starve us to death. We never got near enough food. And when we became sick, there was no medicine.

Of Camp Hitachi, many guards were bullies, a few treated us ok. But the thing that saved lives was "the arrangement" we American officers worked out with the Japanese commander. It was the only camp known that allowed the Americans to run things within the barbed-wire compound. We established the work rosters, and set the schedules. By doing so, we probably angered the guards to no end, but we operated like a unit.

POW Associations and the Last Salute

One afternoon while visiting San Antonio in the summer of 2005, Charlie's younger son, James, was asked by his father to be his guest at a POW Association meeting. These organizations provide support and contact for former POWs. It was a dress-up affair—suits and ties.

A retired Army Air Corps pilot came up and shook hands with James. "You must be Charlie's son," he said, and then introduced himself as retired Colonel Wilson, and shared this brief story:

"I was with your dad in the Philippines during the war. I was a fighter pilot of a P-40 and got into a dogfight with a Japanese Zero. He shot up my plane so badly, I had to bail out somewhere over Luzon. The parachute opened and I was on my way down when the Jap pilot started circling me—for the final kill, I thought.

"There wasn't a darn thing I could do, so I just gave him a final salute.

"The Jap pilot flew so close that I saw him face to face. I was plenty scared. But he never shot me down. Either he was out of bullets or it was an act of professional courtesy. He just let me float down. I'll never forget his face as long as I live.

"Now I'm saluting Charlie. I was in the other prison camp, north. He had been liberated, but instead of going to the safety of our American lines, like everyone else did, he went back and got the rest of the American and Dutch prisoners because he knew where we were. With that train, he brought food and medical supplies and took us back. It was a joy to see him that day. I'll never forget that, either, and I salute him for it. In my view, that is pretty heroic."

Interviews

In the early 1980s, the reunions took on a slightly different tone beginning with the passing of Matt Dobrinic, who had been ill for a long time. Charlie wrote Dobrinic's obituary. In 1992, Eugene Conrad, an even closer friend, died, and Charlie wrote the military part to his obituary. Art Christensen died in 2004—and Charlie wrote in his obituary that he was a great soldier and leader who had negotiated the "agreement" with the Japanese camp commander in 1944, to allow the U.S. officers to run their camp the way they wanted within the barbed wire. Charlie was convinced that action saved lives. By 2006, Charlie was the last officer of the Hitachi Camp POWs still alive. The only remaining friend of that era was former Captain Johnny Olson of POW Camp O'Donnell, who did not go to Hitachi.

In early November 2006, at age 89, Charlie wrote one final obituary—his own. He kept it simple, only writing that he was a POW after the fall of Bataan. He died several weeks later on November 23, 2006. Colonel Charlie Underwood was buried with full military honors in November 2006 at Fort Sam Houston, Texas.

Colonel Charlie Underwood, as a captain, was awarded the Bronze Star with Oak Leaf Cluster for heroism and bravery displayed during the Philippine Campaign, in part due to his unparalleled diligence to save the lives of many POWs while placing himself in harm's way at Camp Hitachi #8B, and his train ride to other camps to assist in liberating POWs. Among his other medals are the Legion of Merit with Oak Leaf Cluster, the Purple Heart, with cluster, the Philippine Presidential Unit World War II Victory Medal, and the Combat Infantry Badge. See Figure 21

Figure 21: Medals

Figure 22: Col. Underwood's funeral caisson

Bibliography

1. Underwood, Major Charles C. "The Defense of Luzon and Bataan, 7 December – 9 April 1942"; 75 pgs. Infantry Officer Advance Course TISL, Fort Benning, GA,1947.

2. Bailey, Jennifer L. "Fall of the Philippines," Center of Military History, Pub 72-3, 1972.

3. Report of Operations of South Luzon Force, Bataan Defense Force & Philippine Corps.

4. Report of Operations of North Luzon Force I Philippine Corps.

5. Report of Operations of United States Armed Forces in Far East, United States Forces in Philippines.

6. Report of Operations of Luzon Forces.

7. Report of Operations of 31st Division, Philippine Army.

8. Report of Operations of 57th Infantry Regiment, Philippine Scouts.

9. War with Japan, Par 1, Dept. of Military Art and Engineering, USMA, August 1945.

10. Wainwright, General Jonathan M. *General Wainwright's Story*. Doubleday Dell, 1946.

11. Lieutenant Colonel Allison. *Bataan: The Judgment Seat.* Macmillan, 1944.

Bibliography

12. Japanese Land Operations, U.S. General Staff (Military Intelligence Service), November 1942.

13. "Bataan," by 1Lt W.F. Hogaboon, Marine Gazette, April, 1946

14. The Fall of the Philippines, by Col. Andrez Lopez, Military Review, August 1946

15. Epic of Corregidor-Bataan, by Lt. Commander T.C. Parker, U.S. Naval Institute Proceedings, May 1942

16. Fighting 26th, by Captain John Wheeler, Cavalry Journal, March- April 1943.

17. Rearguard in Luzon, by Clarke Lee, Cavalry Journal, March-April 1943.

18. Philippine Campaign, Lt.Col. C. Station Babcock, Cavalry Journal, Mar-Apr 1943.

19. Corregidor cable No. 79, By Mel Jacoby, Field Artillery Review, April 1942.

20. Time Magazine, Issues December 1941, June 1942.

21. "O'Donnell-Andersonville of The Pacific," by John E. Olson, Col (ret) Pub. By Olson, 1986

22. "Bataan Our Last Ditch," by Lt. Col. John W. Whitman Hippocrene Books, Inc. NY, NY, 1990

23. "Ghost Soldiers," by Hampton Sides, Double Day NY, NY, 2001

24. Wikipedia "Battle of Bataan," WWW. Wikipedia.Org

25. "Dark Side of the Rising Sun" 1987 circa, a monograph Story of Earl R. Short, with diary sections and comments from

A. Christensen, C. Underwood, et al., Truman Library, Mo.

26. "The Fall of the Philippines," by Luis Morton, Center of Military History, pub 5-2, 1953

27. WWW. 31st Infantry.org/recovery of the Shanghai bowl

28. Ginn, John L. *Sugamo Prison, Tokyo: An Account of the Trial and Sentencing of Japanese War Criminals in 1948,*Case Number 166, page 151.(McFarland & Co., Jefferson, North Carolina and London, 1992).

Bibliography

Appendix I:

Charging documents of guards of Hitachi POW Camp

GENERAL HEADQUARTERS
SUPREME COMMANDER FOR THE ALLIED POWERS

****

BEFORE A MILITARY COMMISSION CONVENED BY THE COMMANDING GENERAL, UNITED STATES EIGHTH ARMY	)))))	UNITED STATES OF AMERICA VS SYOKEI MATSUO

****

CHARGE

That the following member of the Imperial Japanese Army, with his then known title:

Syokei MATSUO, First Lieutenant,

at the times and places set forth in the specifications hereto attached, and during a time of war between the United States of America, its Allies and Dependencies, and Japan, did violate the Laws and Customs of War.

Appendix I

SPECIFICATIONS

1. That from about 3 October 1944 to 7 June 1942, at Tokyo Area Prisoner of War Branch Camp Number 8, also known as Tokyo Area Prisoner of War Dispatch Camp Number 12, Hitachi, Honshu, Japan, the accused, Syokei Matsuo, did unlawfully disregard and fail to discharge his duty as Commander of said Camp by compelling and permitting Allied Prisoners of War to perform excessive and arduous labor, in many cases when they were ill, diseased, and physically unfit to perform such labor and by otherwise mistreating and abusing them, thereby causing the deaths of Thomas J. Hagemaar, Hugo Edwards van Muijen, Theodore A. Doornweerd, Raymond J. Bree, and Ede Groot, Dutch Prisoners of War.

2. That from 3 October 1944 to 7 June 1945, at Tokyo Area Prisoner of War Branch Camp Number 8, also known as Tokyo Area Prisoner of War Dispatch Camp Number 12, Hitachi, Honshu, Japan, the accused, Syokei Matsuo, did unlawfully disregard and fail to discharge his duty as Commander of said Camp by permitting filthy and unhealthful conditions to exist in or about said camp.

3. That from about 3 October 1944 to 7 June 1945, at Tokyo Area Prisoner of War Branch Camp Number 8, also known as Tokyo Area Prisoner of War Dispatch Camp Number 12, Hitachi, Honshu, Japan, the accused Syokei Matsuo, did unlawfully disregard and fail to discharge his duty as Commander of said Camp by withholding and failing to provide Allied Prisoners of War with proper and adequate food, clothing, quarters, heat, medicine and other facilities.

4. That from about 3 October 1944 to 7 June 1945, at Tokyo Area Prisoner of War Branch Camp Number 8, also known as Tokyo Area Prisoner of War Dispatch Camp Number 12, Hitachi, Honshu, Japan, the accused, Syokei Matsuo, did unlawfully disregard and fail to discharge his duty as Commander of said camp by withholding and diverting to his own use Red Cross and other supplies intended for the use and benefit of Allied Prisoners of War.

5. That from about 3 October 1944 to 7 June 1945, at Tokyo Area Prisoner of War Branch Camp Number 8, also known as Tokyo Area Prisoner of War Dispatch Camp Number 12, Hitachi, Honshu, Japan, the accused, Syokei Matsuo, did unlawfully disregard and fail to discharge his duty as Commander of said camp by threatening to impose severe punishment upon any Allied Prisoners of War who might complain to officials concerning offenses committed against said prisoners.

6. That from 3 October 1944 to 7 June 1945, at Tokyo Area Prisoner of War Branch Camp Number 8, also known as Tokyo Area Prisoner of War Dispatch Camp Number 12, Hitachi, Honshu, Japan, the accused, Syokei Matsuo, did willfully and unlawfully mistreat, torture, abuse and beat numerous Allied Prisoners of War.

7. That from 3 October 1944 to 7 June 1945, at Tokyo Area Prisoner of War Branch Camp Number 8, also known as Tokyo Area Prisoner of War Dispatch Camp Number 12, Hitachi, Honshu, Japan, the accused, Syokei Matsuo, did unlawfully disregard and fail to discharge his duty as Commander of said Camp to restrain members of his command and persons under his supervision and control, by permitting them to commit the following cruel and brutal acts, atrocities, and other offenses against certain Allied Prisoners of War:

   a. In or about April 1945, the unlawful mistreatment by Saburo Kozawa, Masatomo Kikuchi, Minrou Fujimoto, and others of Warrant Officer Joseph Reardon, an American Prisoner of War, by beating him into unconsciousness, by forcing him to stand at attention for several hours while holding a bucket of water in each hand, and by otherwise abusing him.

b. In or about December 1944, the unlawful mistreatment by Saburo Kozawa of L. Van Viniren, a Dutch Prisoner of War, by kicking and beating him into unconsciousness and by otherwise abusing him.

c. In or about February 1945, the unlawful mistreatment by Saburo Kozawa of numerous Dutch Prisoners of War, some of whom were suffering from colds and pneumonia, by compelling them to repeatedly immerse their heads and limbs in snow and by otherwise abusing them.

d. On or about 15 November 1944, the unlawful mistreatment by Saburo Kozawa of Luther A. Farrester, an American Prisoner of War, by beating and by otherwise abusing him.

e. On or about 20 April 1945, and on or about 2 June 1945, the unlawful mistreatment by Saburo Kozawa of Lamar A. Bryan, an American Prisoner of War, by beating and by otherwise abusing him.

f. On or about 15 April 1945, the unlawful mistreatment by Saburo Kozawa of Holley L. Wilkinson, an American Prisoner of War, by beating and otherwise abusing him.

g. In or about February 1945, the unlawful mistreatment by Saburo Kozawa of Holley L. Wilkinson, an American Prisoner of War, by burning him.

h. On or about 13 May 1945, the unlawful mistreatment by Saburo Kozawa of T. F. Wilson, an American Prisoner of War, by beating and otherwise abusing him.

i. On or about 14 November 1944, the unlawful mistreatment by Saburo Kozawa of numerous Allied Prisoners of War by causing them to stand at attention for several hours in very cold weather while insufficiently clothed, by clubbing and kicking them, then compelling other Allied Prisoners of War to beat them with fists, and by otherwise abusing them.

j. On or about 15 January 1945, the unlawful mistreatment by Saburo Kozawa of Thomas E. Buchanan, an American Prisoner of War, and numerous other Allied Prisoners of War, by beating them with a club about their heads, then compelling them to hit each other, and by otherwise abusing them.

k. On or about March 1945, the unlawful mistreatment by Saburo Kozawa of Pink Holvey, an American Prisoner of War, by beating and otherwise abusing him.

l. On or about 15 May 1945, the unlawful mistreatment by Saburo Kozawa of Roland Oliviera, a British Prisoner of War, by beating and otherwise abusing him.

m. On or about 15 December 1944, the unlawful mistreatment by Saburo Kozawa of Tan Kay Choon, a British Prisoner of War, by beating and otherwise abusing him.

n. On or about March 1945, the unlawful mistreatment by Saburo Kozawa of Cyril Raymond Togjon, a British Prisoner of War, by beating and otherwise abusing him.

o. On or about 24 May 1945, the unlawful mistreatment by Saburo Kozawa of Gerard Van Galen, a Dutch Prisoner of War, by beating him, compelling him to climb a steep hill twice daily for several days while suffering from an injured foot, and by otherwise abusing him.

p. On or about 8 May 1945, the unlawful mistreatment by Saburo Kozawa of Johannes Ridder and Abram Reiring, Dutch Prisoners of War, by beating them, by depriving them of their Red Cross food supply, and by otherwise abusing them.

3

Appendix I

q. On or about 14 May 1945, the unlawful mistreatment by Saburo Kozawa of William Pieter Van Wingen, a Dutch Prisoner of War, by beating and otherwise abusing him.

r. On or about 15 March 1945, the unlawful mistreatment by Saburo Kozawa of Norman T. Rees, an American Prisoner of War, by beating and otherwise abusing him.

s. In or about May 1945, the unlawful mistreatment by several unidentified guards of Captain Earl Short, Captain Charles Underwood, and Captain William Nealson, American Prisoners of War, by severely beating them with fists, and by otherwise abusing them.

t. In or about April 1945, the unlawful mistreatment by Masatomo Kikuchi of Major James H. Bahrenburg, an American Prisoner of War, by beating and otherwise abusing him.

u. On or about 12 April 1945, the unlawful mistreatment by Masatomo Kikuchi of Charles W. Coombs, an American Prisoner of War, by beating and otherwise abusing him.

v. On or about 15 December 1944 and 20 March 1945, the unlawful mistreatment by Masatomo Kikuchi of Vaandrug Gervardinck, a Dutch Prisoner of War, by beating him and otherwise abusing him.

w. On or about 12 February 1945, the unlawful mistreatment by Toshio Mizuno of Major J. H. Bahrenburg, Captain Charles C. Underwood, and Lieutenant J. I. Renka, Jr., American Prisoners of War, by beating and otherwise abusing them.

x. On or about 12 February 1945, the unlawful mistreatment by Toshio Mizuno of Fred A. Douglas, R. M. Stark, and John P. Dick, American Prisoners of War, W. F. H. Von der Bruggen, A. J. Brosinga, K. L. Gabriel, N. Floor, and H. W. Dernsoiffer, Dutch Prisoners of War, M. Veeramuther and Kee Fah Ten, British Prisoners of War, all of whom were then sick, by ignoring the order of the Japanese doctor that they be given light camp duty and, instead, forcing them to do heavier labor involving the climbing of a steep hill, thereby aggravating the illnesses from which they were suffering, and by otherwise abusing them.

y. On or about 7 February 1945, the unlawful mistreatment by Toshio Mizuno of Holley L. Wilkinson, and American Prisoner of War, and William De Gruiter, Pieter Van Winger and G. Von Galen, Dutch Prisoners of War, by igniting balls of cotton saturated with alcohol upon their flesh, as a result of which they suffered severe burns.

z. Between 1 December 1944 and 28 February 1945, the unlawful mistreatment by Toshio Mizuno of numerous Allied Prisoners of War by compelling them to stand in the snow in severely cold weather for several hours while inadequately clothed and forcing them to beat each other with their fists, and by otherwise abusing them.

aa. On or about 10 February 1945, the unlawful mistreatment by Minrou Fujimoto of William C. Gonyo, an American Prisoner of War, by striking him in the face with a rifle butt, and by otherwise abusing him.

bb. In or about November 1944, the unlawful mistreatment by Minrou Fujimoto of Donald H. Kedzie, an American Prisoner of War, by hitting him with a club, and by otherwise abusing him.

cc. Between 3 October 1944 and 7 June 1945, the unlawful misappropriation of Red Cross and other supplies intended for the use and benefit of Allied Prisoners of War.

SPECIFICATIONS

dd. Between 3 October 1944 and 7 June 1945, the unlawful mistreatment, torture, abuse and beatings of numerous Allied Prisoners of War.

27 January 1947 ~~1946~~ /s/ Alva C. Carpenter
ALVA C. CARPENTER
Chief, Legal Section
General Headquarters
Supreme Commander for the Allied Powers

AFFIDAVIT

Before me personally appeared the above named accuser this **27th** day of **January** 1946, and made oath that he is a person subject to military law and that he personally signed the foregoing charge and specifications and further that he has investigated the matters set forth in the charge and specifications and that the same are true in fact, to the best of his knowledge and belief.

/s/ John R. Pritchard

Captain, Infantry
Summary Court

A CERTIFIED TRUE COPY

CLAUDE A. MUZZY,
C.W.O., U.S.A.

5

Appendix I

Copies for Major Short of 6 accused.

GENERAL HEADQUARTERS
SUPREMEM COMMANDER FOR THE ALLIED POWERS

****

BEFORE A MILITARY COMMISSION CONVENED BY THE COMMANDING GENERAL, UNITED STATES EIGHTH ARMY	)))))	UNITED STATES OF AMERICA VS SABURO KOZAWA

****

CHARGE

That the following civilian guard attached to the Imperial Japanese Army:

Saburo KOZAWA

at the times and places set forth in the specifications hereto attached, and during a time of war between the United States of America, its Allies and Dependencies, and Japan, did violate the Laws and Customs of War.

Deadline—Captain Charlie's Bataan Diary

SPECIFICATIONS

1. That between about 28 September 1944 and 31 August 1945 at Tokyo Area Prisoner of War Branch Camp Number 8, also known as Tokyo Area Prisoner of War Dispatch Camp Number 12, Hitachi, Honshu, Japan, the accused, Saburo Kozawa, with others, did willfully and unlawfully mistreat and torture Allied Prisoners of War by compelling them to perform excessive and arduous labor, in many cases when they were ill, diseased, and physically unfit to perform such labor, and by otherwise mistreating and abusing them, thereby causing the deaths of Thomas J. Hagenaar, Hugo Edwards van Muijen, Theodor A. Doornweerd, Raymond J. Bree, and Ede Groot, Dutch Prisoners of War.

2. That in or about April 1945 at Tokyo Area Prisoner of War Branch Camp Number 8, also known as Tokyo Area Prisoner of War Dispatch Camp Number 12, Hitachi, Honshu, Japan, the accused, Saburo Kozawa, with others, did willfully and unlawfully mistreat Warrant Officer Joseph Reardon, an American Prisoner of War, by beating him into unconsciousness several times, by causing him to stand at attention for several hours while holding a bucket of water in each hand, and by otherwise abusing him.

3. That on or about 28 June 1945, at Tokyo Area Prisoner of War Branch Camp Number 8, also known as Tokyo Area Prisoner of War Dispatch Camp Number 12, Hitachi, Honshu, Japan, the accused, Saburo Kozawa, with others, did willfully and unlawfully mistreat Jean A. Guiraud, an American Prisoner of War, by beating him into unconsciousness and then over a long period of time alternately reviving and beating him into unconsciousness again and by otherwise abusing him.

4. That between 28 September 1944 and 31 August 1945 at Tokyo Area Prisoner of War Branch Camp Number 8, also known as Tokyo Area Prisoner of War Dispatch Camp Number 12, Hitachi, Honshu, Japan, the accused, Saburo Kozawa, did willfully and unlawfully mistreat an unidentified Dutch Prisoner of War by beating him while he was suffering from diarrhea and by otherwise abusing him.

5. That in or about December 1944, at Tokyo Area Prisoner of War Branch Camp Number 8, also known as Tokyo Area Prisoner of War Dispatch Camp Number 12, Hitachi, Honshu, Japan, the accused, Saburo Kozawa, did willfully and unlawfully mistreat L. Van Viniren, a Dutch Prisoner of War, by kicking and beating him into unconsciousness and by otherwise abusing him.

6. That in or about February 1945, at Tokyo Area Prisoner of War Branch Camp Number 8, also known as Tokyo Area Prisoner of War Dispatch Camp Number 12, Hitachi, Honshu, Japan, the accused, Saburo Kozawa, did willfully and unlawfully mistreat numerous Dutch Prisoners of War, some of whom were then suffering from colds and pneumonia, by compelling them to repeatedly immerse their heads and limbs in snow and by otherwise abusing them.

7. That on or about 15 November 1944 at Tokyo Area Prisoner of War Branch Camp Number 8, also known as Tokyo Area Prisoner of War Dispatch Camp Number 12, Hitachi, Honshu, Japan, the accused, Saburo Kozawa, did willfully and unlawfully mistreat Luther A. Farrester, an American Prisoner of War, by beating and by otherwise abusing him.

8. That on or about 20 April 1945 and 2 June 1945, at Tokyo Area Prisoner of War Branch Camp Number 8, also known as Tokyo Area Prisoner of War Dispatch Camp Number 12, Hitachi, Honshu, Japan, the accused, Saburo Kozawa, did willfully and unlawfully mistreat Lamar A. Bryan, an American Prisoner of War, by beating and by otherwise abusing him.

Appendix I

9. That on or about 15 April 1945, at Tokyo Area Prisoner of War Branch Camp Number 8, also known as Tokyo Area Prisoner of War Dispatch Camp Number 12, Hitachi, Honshu, Japan, the accused, Saburo Kozawa, did willfully and unlawfully mistreat Holley L. Wilkinson, an American Prisoner of War, by beating and by otherwise abusing him.

10. That in or about February 1945, at Tokyo Area Prisoner of War Branch Camp Number 8, also known as Tokyo Area Prisoner of War Dispatch Camp Number 12, Hitachi, Honshu, Japan, the accused, Saburo Kozawa, did willfully and unlawfully mistreat and abuse Holley L. Wilkinson, an American Prisoner of War, by igniting bandages applied to his legs, thereby burning him.

11. That on or about 13 May 1945, at Tokyo Area Prisoner of War Branch Camp Number 8, also known as Tokyo Area Prisoner of War Dispatch Camp Number 12, Hitachi, Honshu, Japan, the accused, Saburo Kozawa, did willfully and unlawfully mistreat T. F. Wilson, an American Prisoner of War, by beating and otherwise abusing him.

12. That on or about 14 November 1944, at Tokyo Area Prisoner of War Branch Camp Number 8, also known as Tokyo Area Prisoner of War Dispatch Camp Number 12, Hitachi, Honshu, Japan, the accused, Saburo Kozawa, did willfully and unlawfully mistreat numerous Allied Prisoners of War by causing them to stand at attention for several hours in very cold weather while insufficiently clothed, by clubbing and kicking them and by then compelling other Allied Prisoners of War to beat them with their fists and by otherwise abusing them.

13. That on or about 15 January 1945, at Tokyo Area Prisoner of War Branch Camp Number 8, also known as Tokyo Area Prisoner of War Dispatch Camp Number 12, Hitachi, Honshu, Japan, the accused, Saburo Kozawa, did willfully and unlawfully mistreat Thomas E. Buchanan, an American Prisoner of War, and numerous other Allied Prisoners of War by beating them with a club and then compelling them to strike each other and by otherwise abusing them.

14. That in or about March 1945, at Tokyo Area Prisoner of War Branch Camp Number 8, also known as Tokyo Area Prisoner of War Branch Camp Number 12, Hitachi, Honshu, Japan, the accused, Saburo Kozawa, did willfully and unlawfully mistreat Pink Helvey, an American Prisoner of War, by beating and by otherwise abusing him.

15. That on or about 15 May 1945, at Tokyo Area Prisoner of War Branch Camp Number 8, also known as Tokyo Area Prisoner of War Dispatch Camp Number 12, Hitachi, Honshu, Japan, the accused, Saburo Kozawa, did willfully and unlawfully mistreat Roland Oliviere, a British Prisoner of War, by beating and otherwise abusing him.

16. That on or about 15 December 1944, at Tokyo Area Prisoner of War Branch Camp Number 8, also known as Tokyo Area Prisoner of War Dispatch Camp Number 12, Hitachi, Honshu, Japan, the accused, Saburo Kozawa, did willfully and unlawfully mistreat Tan Kay Choon, a British Prisoner of War, by beating and otherwise abusing him.

17. That in or about March 1945, at Tokyo Area Prisoner of War Branch Camp Number 8, also known as Tokyo Area Prisoner of War Dispatch Camp Number 12, Hitachi, Honshu, Japan, the accused, Saburo Kozawa, did willfully and unlawfully mistreat Cyril Raymond Toggon, a British Prisoner of War, by beating and otherwise abusin him.

18. That on or about 24 May 1945, at Tokyo Area Prisoner of War Branch Camp Number 8, also known as Tokyo Area Prisoner of War Dispatch Camp Number 12, Hitachi, Honshu, Japan, the accused, Saburo Kozawa, did willfully and unlawfully mistreat Gerard Van Galen, a Dutch Prisoner of War, by beating him, compelling him to climb a steep hill twice daily for several days while suffering from an injured foot and by otherwise abusing him.

SPECIFICATIONS - Continued

19. That on or about 8 May 1945, at Tokyo Area Prisoner of War Branch Camp Number 8, also known as Tokyo Area Prisoner of War Dispatch Camp Number 12, Hitachi, Honshu, Japan, the accused, Saburo Kozawa, did willfully and unlawfully mistreat Johannes Ridder and Abram Reiring, Dutch Prisoners of War, by beating them, by depriving them of their Red Cross food supply, and by otherwise abusing them.

20. That on or about 14 May 1945, at Tokyo Area Prisoner of War Branch Camp Number 8, also known as Tokyo Area Prisoner of War Dispatch Camp Number 12, Hitachi, Honshu, Japan, the accused, Saburo Kozawa, did willfully and unlawfully mistreat William Pieter Von Wingen, a Dutch Prisoner of War, by beating and by otherwise abusing him.

21. That on or about 15 March 1945, at Tokyo Area Prisoner of War Branch Camp Number 8, also known as Tokyo Area Prisoner of War Dispatch Camp Number 12, Hitachi, Honshu, Japan, the accused, Saburo Kozawa, did willfully and unlawfully mistreat Norman T. Rees, an American Prisoner of War, by beating and otherwise abusing him.

22. That between 28 September 1944 and 31 August 1945, at Tokyo Area Prisoner of War Branch Camp Number 8, also known as Tokyo Area Prisoner of War Dispatch Camp Number 12, Hitachi, Honshu, Japan, the accused, Saburo Kozawa, with others, did willfully and unlawfully mistreat William L. Phillips, an American Prisoner of War, by beating and by otherwise abusing him.

23. That between 28 September 1944 and 31 August 1945, at Tokyo Area Prisoner of War Branch Camp Number 8, also known as Tokyo Area Prisoner of War Dispatch Camp Number 12, the accused, Saburo Kozawa, did willfully mistreat, torture, beat and otherwise abuse numerous American and Allied Prisoners of War.

27 January 1947

/s/ Alva C. Carpenter
ALVA C. CARPENTER
Chief, Legal Section
General Headquarters
Supreme Commander for the Allied Powers

AFFIDAVIT

Before me personally appeared the above named accuser this 27th day of January 1947, and he made oath that he is a person subject to military law and that he personally signed the foregoing charge and specifications and further that he had investigated the matters set forth in the charge and specifications and that the same are true in fact, to the best of his knowledge and belief.

/s/ John R. Pritchard

Captain, Infantry
Summary Court

A CERTIFIED TRUE COPY

/s/ Claude A. Muzzy

CLAUDE A. MUZZY
C.W.O., U.S.A.

Appendix II:

Enclosed is part of a report Captain Underwood submitted to the War Crimes Commission regarding the nutrition of the POWs.

Deadline—Captain Charlie's Bataan Diary

If one thing could be singled out as having the most important bearing on the welfare of a Japanese prisoner of war, it would be food.

Acting as inside camp administrators, American officers, largely on their own initiative, did wonders in personnel and camp sanitation, morale, discipline and the other phases of interned life. But in most cases commanding officers' chief problem was trying to get the Japanese to issue enough food.

Both in the Philippines and Japan where I was interned since the fall of Bataan, I know one could look at the ration figures for a few months and tell the conditions of the men without even seeing them. Ironically enough an adequate medicine supply seemed to parallel a proper food ration. In the early days of internment at Camp O'Donnel, Philippines, where men were dying nearly as fast as they could be buried, there was neither proper food nor medicine. An adequate supply of quinine in those early days, however, would have saved the lives of most, at least for the time being.

With approximately 900 out of 5000 dying in one month at our second camp, Cabanatuan, Philippines, this was also true. After about six months as prisoners even the Japanese doctors said the men were slowly starving to death.

Appendix II

2

Then we started getting a comparative adequate diet- daily meat (about 100 grams a man) and sufficient rice and vegetables. Simultaneously a large shipment of medicine, particularly quinine was received. Soon we had a "deathless day". With Red Cross food and medicine arriving at Christmas, we began looking "alive" again.

Later at Japan, in my camp, Tokyo Dispatch No. 12, after a tough trip from Cabanatuan and two or three months of short rations, many men had lost considerable weight and were in weakened condition again. There was enough medicine here but food was insufficient for the men to gain back their former weight. This report, however, is not to survey prison life since internment. Its purpose is to picture food conditions at an average Japanese work camp. It covers a period August 23, 1944, to February 20, 1945 when I was mess officer at this camp.

One of eight officers, and 292 enlisted men, I left the Philippines in March 1944 for Japan. Entire detail was examined repeatedly by the Japanese and was in comparatively good health.

About four months after arrival, I relieved Capt. E. B. Conrad, an able man, as mess officer. By this time, Americans remaining had lost considerable weight and were generally in a weakened condition. This is attributed to the inadequate diet for the amount of manual labor required of the men. They were doing hard work in a copper mine, the type which would merit a balanced diet of at least 4500 calories under sufficient animal protein.

WAR CRIMES OFFICE
Washington 25, D. C.

Men coming from other similar camps to replace 250 Americans removed because "too many Americans close to the sea coast were dangerous" were also for the most part in poor condition. Of 150 Dutch troops from Camp 8- Dutch, Javenese, and Dutch Jaenese- many were in pitiful shape. Eighty British Royal Air Force Colonial troops from Camp 2- Chinese, Indians and Eurasians, originally from Malaya- were younger and smaller, averaging 23 years old. They were comparatively in good shape- better than the Americans and Dutch. For period covered herein, all maintained about the same weight as when they came here. (See appendix B) Five American officers remaining - on same diet as the men- followed the general pattern. Of four deaths during the winter, all were Dutch.

As mess officer, my dealings were directly with the Japanese- drawing rations and fuel, food preparations, man-power also. Nominally there was a retired Japanese private soldier, a Kozowa by name, in charge of the kitchen and storehouse. He allowed me virtual freedom in preparation of food and kitchen management.

This man's knowledge of his job was far below that required of the average American mess sergeant or cook. He knew nothing of body requirements for necessary foods. He had no understanding of calories, proteins, vitamines, etc. Also was he equally at a loss in storehouse management.

My dealings theoritically were through him and a civilian in charge of supplies furnished by the mining company- vegetables, meat and fish- to the camp commander. This officer was first a captain of the Japanese regular army and then a first lieutenant called up from retirement.

WAR CRIMES OFFICE
Washington 25, D. C.

Appendix II

4

Although nominally the kitchen was not under supervision of the American camp commander, first Maj. A. G. Christensen then Capt. E. R. Short, we worked together harmoniously at all times. Repeatedly we conversed with the Japanese commander to secure more food with varying results. I believe the real gauge of food issued above a certain minumum was the camp work sheet. When a great number of men missed work, particularly through weakness, the diet increased for a while. As the men improved it would fall back. It seemed we could never convince the Japanese they would achive more from their standpoint - more **men working and less medicine expended, - if** they would feed us properly.

As well as I could determine we were supposed to receive a basic ration something like this per man: main food (rice, coryon, barley and soy beans) 705 grams, vegetables of all (or any) kinds 500 grams, salt .05 grams, sugar 10 grams, meso (a salty soy bean paste) 75 grams, shoyu (a seasoning sauce) 60 grams. Then what meat or fish, condiments, cooking oil, red beans, flour, etc. which came in was additional.

We received usually enough under this to feed the Japan administration personnel assigned to the camp. This left main food about 690, vegetables 300 to 400, salt, .04, sugar, (when we got it which was about 2/3 of the time) .05 to .07, meso 70 and shoyu 55. We supplied the Japanese kitchen with these later two items as well as vegetables occassionally. Often the vegetables issue would not materialize so this item fell below the standard.

Stock answer to my complaint of food shortage under prescribed amount was a certain amount deducted to cover breakage and spoilage,

I knew sugar was being stolen but I could never be sure about the others. Often when stores were inventoried at end of the month, we would receive slight additional grain, meso and shoyu, but seldom sugar from surplus which was on hand for the month completed.

With this ration, a day's meals went something like this: large bowl (soup size) of steamed grain and a tea bowl of thin vegetables soup for breakfast. At noon grain was the same and seasoned vegetables cooked dry as the men had to carry a lunch and eat cold food. Sometimes they had a pickle, some meso paste, or piece of fish. Supper meal was grain and usually vegetable soup. Sometimes fish or meat, or an extra vegetable side dish could be served. If fuel was sufficient, tea was given at breakfast or supper. Japanese considered soy beans as part of the main food and wanted it cooked in the grain. The beans would not get soft thoroughly this way. We convinced them the men preferred beans made into a soup with shoyu or meso and we were allowed to serve them this way for supper.

Supply of beans ran out December 15. Nearly 90 grams per man which were issued was made up in grain. As beans contained oil and protein in large quantity, this loss was felt keenly.

During most of this time we had no cooking oil or lard. Condiments, which were insufficient and spasmodic, were a little pepper and some fish or curry powder for soup.

Had we received enough meat and fish and the soy beans continued, I believe the men would have fared all right. Vegetables through the winter pleasantly surprised me. We received enough daily for some sort of dish although it was large radishes for more than a month during January. But also in the winter we had fresh carrots, greens, spring onions, potatoes and gobo (a root). Rest of the year, vege-

Appendix II

tables were of good quality- tomatoes, squash, cucumbers, egg plant, green beans, etc. Seldom would we get much variety at one time. Maybe three days' ration of egg plant, or another day- tomatoes, or four days' cucumbers would come in.

In the fall we received many sweet potatoes. Japanese attempted to replace kilo for kilo Irish and sweet potatoes for grain, one meal out of six for about a month. I finally convinced them, on their own figures, **grain was** about 360 calories per 100 grams whereas sweet potatoes were 139 and **Irish** 94. Thus the men were not getting as much to eat. They compromised by giving me twice as many kilos sweet potatoes as the **grain they replaced**, saying they had to get rid of the potatoes before they spoiled.

In appendix A are given statistics covering calories and such. These are taken from daily records I kept. During the entire period our daily caloric average was 3054 with 12 6/7 per cent protein per man. Luckily when soy beans were discontinued in December, fish and meat started coming in again. Also we received Red Cross food packages which helped considerably. On December 22 we got one small box per man and again on January 18, plus some the Japanese gave as prizes. (This was extent of Red Cross food during this six months period.)

One was unable to buy food stuffs through prisoners' canteen here. In the Philippines our diet was augmented considerable from this source.

Actually we received less main food for sick persons- 570 grams per man- but we feed everyone the same ration. Many men were unable to eat steamed grain. For these we substituted a soupy rice, similar to Filipino lugao, made from polished rice, which was easier to digest.

Deadline—Captain Charlie's Bataan Diary

On September 11, we moved into a new and better kitchen. An oven was completed on December 12. We then began baking bread which was substituted in part for grain. During the entire time we were serving a poor grade of yeast drink to sick men. This was built up and used for raising agent in the bread. Occasionally before we had baked bread in small self-made pans whenever we would get flour. About a month after the oven came a grinder of sorts and we could grain for bread.

The oven was a great help in food preparation. For a short time Japanese insisted we serve bread instead of grain at each meal. Bread was of course none too good. For one thing sugar for yeast was insufficient and grain could not be ground finely enough. But most men liked the change. The Japanese considered bread some sort of "cure all" and we had to serve it until the grinder broke. Before the oven came the Japanese had their first bread craze and we steamed it.

As was true of most Japanese equipment, it looked good, but would not stand up under usage. The grinder was in repair as much as in operation. Pots, buckets, paddles, everything would fall apart in a short time.

Cooking was done in cast iron pots. We had two stoves which were large concrete-brick affairs with four fire boxes in each. Above each fire box was an opening in which the pot fitted with a flu for each two stoves in the rear.

Best thing about the kitchen was the oven. - it was made from our own specifications. Food was placed into buckets and distributed to individual rooms - 14 to 16 men each.

Water supply was plentiful. Electric light were good. Two of the three meals had to be cooked at night because of an early breakfast (5 a.m.) and lunches to be carried to work. Night shift naturally had

Appendix II

different hours. Some difficulty was experienced during blackouts.

During winter months we had a fuel problem. Many meals had to be prepared in a way to save fuel rather than to cook food most appetizingly in order to get it cooked on the fuel alloted. For more than a month we burned nothing but brush. Many of the cooks could not complete their shift because of blindness. They would rest right after cooking. They would be all right after resting.

When I first took over the kitchen, I had a crew of nine men of mixed nationalities. Five were good cooks in fine physical condition. The other four were sick men to help out and who needed work in the kitchen, the Japanese said, to make them well. Gradually the Japanese replaced the well men with sick ones - until all were unfit for mine duty. Some were cooks and we got along all right. Then the crew was changed back to six well men and I was allowed, as long as I selected no men in key mine jobs, to pick my own men - two of each nationality. With either the original nine or the six well men, the kitchen operated smoothly.

Dishonesty on part of Japanese was present, but I think not excessive compared to their normal "cut" in anything they handle. See Appendix C. Their thefts were confined to stores in charge of Japanese and not to cooked food. I refused all demands of food by the individual guards and backed up by the camp commander on my stand.

In regards to treatment, the kitchen was left alone fairly much by the sentries, except when they were refused food. Of course we all had to salute Japanese even if we were working. Failure to do so resulted in beatings. My policy was to stay as business-like as possible with all Japanese and avoid all familiarities. This proved best in the long run.

Although my arguments with the Japanese were numerous, only on one occasion was I manhandled. See Appendix D.

In relieving me, the Japanese officer expressed appreciation for my services. He explained his policy was to change officers in their administrative duties about every six months. But the real reason I was changed, I am sure, was that the local administration resented my "stepping on their toes." At an inspection by a Japanese colonel commanding the tokyo dispatch camps, this man allowed me to voice any complaints I might have. I told him the men were hungry, they were not getting enough to eat for the amount of work they were doing. Particularly insufficient was meat and fish. Also was included discontinuance of soy beans, no cooking oil or lard and scarce condiments and fuel problems. (At the time we were burning brush). He told me we should receive 2500 calories a day. And I heard him tell the camp commander to get us coal and he also inquired about soy beans and fish. Immediately our diet picked up somewhat and remained comparatively good for the few weeks I remained in the kitchen.

RATION REPORT

ADD 1   Sept. 4, 1945

On February 20, John I. Renka, 2nd. Lt., A. C., relieved me as mess officer.

Conditions in kitchen remained generally about the same. Monthly food reports, similar to one I have submitted above, were destroyed by Lt. Renka. (The Japanese camp officials, after the surrender, ordered all records kept by the prisoners destroyed. They burned all of theirs likewise. My foregoing report was buried shortly after it was written. This, together with another one on mal-treatment, came out of hiding only today.) I shall consolidate Lt. Renka's material into monthly reports as well as I can from a day by day journal which he did not destroy.

Generally it is safe to say, food, during the past six months, has been barely enough to sustain life under these conditions. Many deficiency diseases were present. As the war was brought closer to us day by day, the Japanese either couldn't or wouldn't supply us with a decent vegetable ration. Issues were spasmodic and incomplete. Fish and meat ceased.

Appendix II

-19-

On July 17, mining installations in nearby Motayama and Hitachi were damaged by bombs. From then on only about one half of the men in camp worked at the mine. And the mining company virtually ceased to supply us with food stuffs.

We organized hiking expeditions, and weather permitting, searched nearby mountains and valleys for wild grass and weeds which were edible after a fashion. They were made into a soup.

After we had taken over virtual control of camp about August 27, Capt. Short appointed me mess officer again.

By this time, the Japanese were giving us anything they could. Soon after their surrender, they gave us all the grain we could eat, obtained grease and vegetables and increased issue of such items as sugar and beans. When I took over, there was no food problem. We had received two large food drops from Army B-29's. Also weather permitting, Navy fliers paid us at least a daily visit, dropping small rations of canned goods, coffee, etc.

These past two weeks, of course, have been the happiest of our prison life. The men were getting all they could eat. There was no interference by Japanese. We fed three big meals a day-- each one all a man wanted- with hot chocolate call at 9 and 8 p.m. From surrender until now, many men have gained between 15 and 20 pounds. One could hardly recognize the former human scare-crows of a month ago.

Appendix A. - Food statistics.

August: Calories, 3102, per cent protein, 13.6. Meat, 5 times (twice intestines) for 462 grams per man. Freash fish 8 times for 1204 grams, dried fish 15 times for 596 grams.

September: Calories 2839, per cent protein 15.1. Meat once for 207 grams per man. Fresh fish 5 times for 560 grams per man. Dried fish 8 times for 192 grams per man.

October: Calories 3054, per cent protein 14.2. Meat 3 times (all intestines) for 251 grams. Fresh fish 4 times for 575 grams per man.

November: 3198 calories, protein 11.7. Meat 3 times (intestines 2) for 200 grams. Fresh fish 9 times for 223 grams. Dried fish 2 times for 89 grams per man.

December: 2845 calories, protein 10.7 . Meat 5 times (all intestines) for 537 grams. Fresh fish 8 times for 223 grams, Dried fish 10 times for 443 grams per man.

-11-

January: Calories 3094. Protein 9.5 %. Meat 9 times (once intestines) for 221 grams. Fresh fish 19 times for 1488. Fish cakes, (ground fish and meal made into a cake somewhat like dog biscuits) 25 times for 2747 grams per man.

February: Calories 3010, Protein 9.8%. Meat twice for 62 grams. Blood (dried) twice for 169 grams. Fresh fish 19 times for 1473 grams. Fish cakes once for 156 grams. Dried fish once for 14 grams. Fish powder 8 times for 379 grams per man.

Total average 3054   Protein 126/7 %

Pages which follow are day by day food consumption sheets for each month.

Appendix B.   Weight statistics.

	Americans	Dutch	British	Average
August	63.12	57.63	56.84	59.093
Sept.	63.14	58.12	55.61	58.303
Oct.	62.69	56.43	55.09	58.050
Nov.	64.21	57.27	56.14	59.211
Dec.	64.63	58.85	54.49	59.320
Jan.	64.31	57.36	55.21	58.956

(Nearly 10 per cent of the command had "wet" beri-beri during the last three months and were considerably swollen with water.)

Average American weight on leaving Cabanatuan, P.I. - 72.87
Average American weight on arriving Japan camp - 65.44

Appendix C.   Report on dishonesty.

Japanese in charge of rations, Nozowa, showed one figure on records he kept regarding his issues to me. In many cases we actually received less. This is particularly true on sugar. Following is an excerpt from my records. November, 1944.

Date	Jap. record show	Actually received
13	Sugar 2,940 grams	500 grams
14	" "	"
15	" "	"

Appendix II

-15-

(continuation)

16	sugar 2,960 grams –	500 grams
	rice 39 kilos	30 kilo
17	thru 21 same on sugar	
21	sugar same, rice 28 kilo	25 kilo
22	thru 25 same on sugar	
26	sugar same, rice 39 kilo	35 kilo
27	sugar same	
28	sugar same rice 38 kilo	30 kilo
29	sugar same rice 40	35 kilo
	salt 1.48	1 kilo
30	sugar same rice 39 kilo	30 kilo

December 1944.
1 to 12 sugar same
13, 14, 15 sugar 2,960   1,500
15   sugar 2.960   2,000
15 thru 29 same.
30 and 31 sugar 2.960   none.

(more)

The above is only an example. Similar instances were experienced throughout. Rice was only grain greatly shorted and sugar the other big item.

Individual thefts. On all these cases I have proper witnesses.

On November 18, Kozowa took approximately 3 kilos of sugar (three) from locker in store room. He placed it in a blue sack and took it out of camp. Seen by Boey, 265 and Chan 239.

On December 19, Kozowa took approximately two kilos of fish powder, one kilo of sea weed and one kilo of sugar from storehouse and took it out of camp. Seen by Boey 265.

On January 6, Kozowa took approximately an American cigar box (50 size) full of dried fish from storehouse and took out of camp.

On November 6, 1944, Kozowa took from storehouse and sent out of camp to campcommander's house 1st. Lieut. Sokei Matsuo, approximately five kilos of onions, three kilos of carrots and three kilos of radishes. Seen by Boey 265 and Chan 239.

On November 27 approximately 10 kilos of radishes and on December 21 seven kilos of turnips, were taken from storehouse by Kozowa and carried by Japanese office boy, Sawada to home of 1st. Lieut Sokei Matsuo.

WAR CRIMES OFFICE

Deadline—Captain Charlie's Bataan Diary

Feb. 4, 1945, onions three kilos and potatoes seven kilos and on Feb. 20, carrots, four kilos, onions five kilos and radishes, three kilos were taken from kitchen store house by Kozowa and carried by Sawada to Matsuo's house. Seen by Kinsey, 22 and Coombs, 48.

On January 2, 1945, Corporal Tosho Mizuno came into the kitchen storehouse and carried away about three kilos of onions. Seen by Bosy 265 and Cooms 48.

All the above cases I have seen myself as well as others mentioned. Regardless if the items were taken from the kitchen storehouse or the general storehouse, it indirectly came out of the prisoners' ration. If there was any shortage, it was taken from prisoners' issue and not shorted from Japanese.

Appendix D. Mistreatment.

On the evening of Feb. 12, 1945, Cpl. Tosho Mizuno, Japanese second in command was taking evening roll call in the kitchen. He questioned me about some garlic. He asked why I did not issue any raw for supper for that evening as he had told me to do. I explained that day's issue had been used in food for breakfast and lunch. He said I should use some from that which he personally issued that afternoon. When I told him that was for tomorrow's ration and I was not getting enough for three meals, he flew into a rage, said I was disobeying his orders and cried "bacero" (fool). He then struck me several times in the face with an object similar to an American clip board. Witnesses: entire kitchen crew, particularly Sgt. R. O. Kinsey ASN. 6935012 and Sgt. Charles W. Combs ASN 13017033. It is my desire to prefer charges against Cpl. Mizuno for this offense as well as the items of theft by all mentioned above.

CERTIFIED CORRECT:

Charles C. Underwood
CHARLES C. UNDERWOOD

EARL R. SHORT
Capt. Inf.

STATE OF Kansas) SS
COUNTY OF Shawnee)

I, Charles C. Underwood, Captain, United States Army, being duly sworn on oath, state that I have read the foregoing statement together

WAR CRIMES OFFICE

Appendix III:

Japanese Surrender Documents

Deadline—Captain Charlie's Bataan Diary

INSTRUMENT OF SURRENDER

We, acting by command of and in behalf of the Emperor of Japan, the Japanese Government and the Japanese Imperial General Headquarters, hereby accept the provisions set forth in the declaration issued by the heads of the Governments of the United States, China and Great Britain on 26 July, 1945 at Potsdam, and subsequently adhered to by the Union of Soviet Socialist Republics, which four powers are hereafter referred to as the Allied Powers.

We hereby proclaim the unconditional surrender to the Allied Powers of the Japanese Imperial General Headquarters and of all Japanese armed forces and all armed forces under Japanese control wherever situated.

We hereby command all Japanese forces wherever situated and the Japanese people to cease hostilities forthwith, to preserve and save from damage all ships, aircraft, and military and civil property and to comply with all requirements which may be imposed by the Supreme Commander for the Allied Powers or by agencies of the Japanese Government at his direction.

We hereby command the Japanese Imperial General Headquarters to issue at once orders to the Commanders of all Japanese forces and all forces under Japanese control wherever situated to surrender unconditionally themselves and all forces under their control.

We hereby command all civil, military and naval officials to obey and enforce all proclamations, orders and directives deemed by the Supreme Commander for the Allied Powers to be proper to effectuate this surrender and issued by him or under his authority and we direct all such officials to remain at their posts and to continue to perform their non-combatant duties unless specifically relieved by him or under his authority.

We hereby undertake for the Emperor, the Japanese Government and their successors to carry out the provisions of the Potsdam Declaration in good faith, and to issue whatever orders and take whatever action may be required by the Supreme Commander for the Allied Powers or by any other designated representative of the Allied Powers for the purpose of giving effect to that Declaration.

We hereby command the Japanese Imperial Government and the Japanese Imperial General Headquarters at once to liberate all allied prisoners of war and civilian internees now under Japanese control and to provide for their protection, care, maintenance and immediate transportation to places as directed.

The authority of the Emperor and the Japanese Government to rule the state shall be subject to the Supreme Commander for the Allied Powers who will take such steps as he deems proper to effectuate these terms of surrender.

Appendix III

Signed at **TOKYO BAY, JAPAN** at _09.04 I_
on the **SECOND** day of **SEPTEMBER**, 1945.

重光葵
By Command and in behalf of the Emperor of Japan
and the Japanese Government.

梅津美治郎
By Command and in behalf of the Japanese
Imperial General Headquarters.

Accepted at **TOKYO BAY, JAPAN** at _0908 I_
on the **SECOND** day of **SEPTEMBER**, 1945,
for the United States, Republic of China, United Kingdom and the
Union of Soviet Socialist Republics, and in the interests of the other
United Nations at war with Japan.

Douglas MacArthur
Supreme Commander for the Allied Powers.

C.W. Nimitz
United States Representative

徐永昌
Republic of China Representative

Bruce Fraser
United Kingdom Representative

Derevyanko
Union of Soviet Socialist Republics
Representative

T.A. Blamey
Commonwealth of Australia Representative

Moore-Cosgrave
Dominion of Canada Representative

Leclerc
Provisional Government of the French
Republic Representative

Helfrich
Kingdom of the Netherlands Representative

Isitt
Dominion of New Zealand Representative

Acknowledgments

Acknowledgments for this project go to many: To the defenders of Bataan, one of the most heroic army of soldiers this country has ever produced. To the Descendants Group of the American Defenders of Bataan and Corregidor (ADBC), which produces The Quan, the official magazine for POW descendants: Their editor placed a short article written by this author requesting research on the war crime trials of Yokohama, which then generated information regarding the verdicts against the guards of Hitachi POW Camp. And to an American-Japanese contributor from the Hitachi area, who provided more details of the train route presented at the end of this story.

These invaluable sources enriched Captain Charlie Underwood's story and provided additional material to fill in the gaps. Information obtained through The Center for Research, Allied Prisoners of War under the Japanese at www.pow1@mansel.com, was very useful for providing information about the Hitachi Camp. Finally, Brian Carr, Ph.D., who consolidated related documents about Charlie on a CD, which made it easy to access information about Charlie across the span of forty years. Any financial profit from this book will be donated to associations that support and honor POWs and their families. (This should go at the end of this section.)

For over fifty years, Charlie did not wish to speak of his war experiences. In 2004, he provided a three-hour interview to the author regarding those years. In 2005, his nephew, Brian D. Carr, Ph.D., of Lubbock, Texas, conducted and taped a three-hour interview with Charlie about his war experiences. Dr. Carr later consolidated many related documents, POW witness statements, and newspaper clippings on a CD.

After Charlie's death in late 2006, his children found an old army footlocker in his garage that contained documents pertaining to the war and his years as a POW. Chief among them was a rare 75-page monograph, written by Charlie in 1947, called *The Defense of Luzon and Bataan, December 1941 – April 1942*. One military historian has referred to the monograph as one of the first accounts of the fighting on Luzon and Bataan. Other photos of the war years were found by his daughter and son-in-law, Vickye and Mark Lambdin. Mark, a professional photographer, enhanced photos dating back to the pre-WWII era. These were the sources of the materials used to write this important saga. All the documents recorded by Dr.Carr, titled the "Underwood Papers," are now in the archives of Texas Tech University, in Lubbock, Texas.

About the Author

Charles Underwood, Jr., as the son of a military officer, grew up on various Army posts across the country. He knew many officers in Captain Charlie's Story and made his own judgments of their character and accomplishments. He considers them the modern knights of American society. While developing a deep respect for them, he also keenly observed their struggles and adjustments back into normal life, after release from captivity as a POW.

Charles Jr. is a lifelong student of history; a former distinguished military graduate and a former officer in the Army. He holds a master's degree from the University of Hawaii and a doctorate (Ph.D) from the University of Southern California. He now resides in the Southwest in the winters and summers in New England.

CPSIA information can be obtained
at www.ICGtesting.com
Printed in the USA
LVOW12s1949080518
576441LV00005B/1004/P